HOT ROD
DETAILING

Timothy Remus

Motorbooks International
Publishers & Wholesalers ®

First published in 1993 by Motorbooks International Publishers & Wholesalers, PO Box 2, 729 Prospect Avenue, Osceola, WI 54020 USA

Motorbooks International is a certified trademark, registered with the United States Patent Office

The information in this book is true and complete to the best of our knowledge. All recommendations are made without any guarantee on the part of the author or Publisher, who also disclaim any liability incurred in connection with the use of this data or specific details

We recognize that some words, model names and designations, for example, mentioned herein are the property of the trademark holder. We use them for identification purposes only. This is not an official publication

Motorbooks International books are also available at discounts in bulk quantity for industrial or sales-promotional use. For details write to Special Sales Manager at the Publisher's address

Library of Congress Cataloging-in-Publication Data
Remus, Timothy
    Hot rod detailing / Timothy Remus.
        p.   cm.
    Includes index.
    ISBN 0-87938-703-3
    1. Hot rods.   2. Automobile detailing.   I. Title.
TL236.3.R466   1993
629.228—dc20   92-29759

On the front cover: Jamie Musselman's Model A roadster was originally built by Little John and has been rebuilt and repainted by Hot Rods by Boyd.

Printed and bound in the United States of America

Contents

Acknowledgments

The older I get the more obvious it becomes: You can't do it all alone, be it book writing, car detailing, or whatever.

The list of people who helped with this detailing book starts with Brian Truesdell, a professional pinstriper from St. Paul, Minnesota. Brian let me sit through a morning's work while he mixed paint, explained the ins and outs of pinstriping and then added a stripe to Jim Kalkes' Chevy street rod.

As I became more involved with detailing, I learned that there are some very different opinions on the most basic aspects of car cleaning. I thought it might be interesting to interview people who detail cars for a living. Thus I must thank Scott Lindsey of S&R Detailing in Richfield, Minnesota, for an afternoon of his time and for answering all my varied questions.

During a recent trip to California, I was lucky enough to meet Far-Out Gary, another professional detailer. Gary was recommended to me by Dick Brogdon, the manager of Boyd Coddington's Hot Rod Shop (most of the Boyd-built hot rods are detailed by Gary). Gary consented to an interview and proved to be a man with a wealth of knowledge. For his sharing that knowledge and a few neat tricks, I am most grateful to Gary.

In search of more information on the various products, I decided to let my fingers do the walking.

During the many conversations I had with company owners and representatives, I met more than a few interesting people. One of the most interesting and most generous was Marlene Besa, from One Grand Company. Another was Phil Meyers from Lexol. These two and many others helped with information, products, and photos.

Finally, I have to thank the one man who became essential to the completion of the book. Eric Aurand is a talented artist and illustrator, and a recent graduate of Stout University in Wisconsin. He is also a car nut through and through, and very knowledgeable about the best means for detailing street rods. His detailing knowledge comes from hands-on experience gained while preparing and detailing local street rods for the International Show Car Association (ISCA) winter show. Eric posed for photos, offered advice on the best products, helped find cars for us to detail, and offered his enthusiasm to the project.

Kurt Senescall and Doug Halverson at Creative Metal Metalworks let us use some of their personal toys for demonstration purposes and photos. Thanks.

Finally, I must thank Steve Anderson and Dick Cox, owners of the two very nice street rods seen most often in this book.

Introduction

This book is intended to be a guide for the street rod owner who desires to detail his or her car. By detailing, we mean more than just the process of washing and waxing the car. Detailing means going well beyond the normal cleaning to remove all the dirt and debris that might be in or on the car. Detailing means bringing the paint to a high state of luster and treating it to maintain that luster. Detailing means taking each part of the car and cleaning it as a separate operation. Detailing means doing all the little things that make a difference between a car that has been cleaned up, and one that has been detailed. Ultimately, detailing means making the car look as good as it possibly can—short of a complete paint job and rebuild.

The book breaks down the detailing process into separate sections: the body, the engine, the chassis, the wheels and tires, the interior, and convertible tops. Each is covered separately. Because detailing includes all the little things that make a car look exceptionally good, a section on pinstriping is included.

The individuals who perform any particular task for their living always have a unique and professional perspective and I have included two interviews with professional detailers. One works in a conventional detailing shop while the other works in a small shop at home and limits his work to street rods and classic cars. Both have interesting opinions as to the best products and methods. In the end, however, there is more to be learned from their attitudes than from any one product or method of cleaning.

Some people might question the need for a book on street rod detailing, when the bookshelves and catalogs carry plenty of other, more generic, detailing books. Why a separate book for street rods they ask?

The answer is simple. There is a need for a separate street rod detailing book because street rods are very different from any other automobile. They are essentially hand-built cars, built and maintained for reasons outside the realm of reality for "other" more normal cars.

Street rods carry enormous mechanical detail. The engines don't hide under long hoods but rather are built to be seen and designed to please the eye. The typical street rod chassis (if there is such a thing as a typical chassis) carries far more detail and more chromed and polished components than the chassis on any other type of car.

Cleaning, polishing, and detailing all the mechanical detail requires different methods and products than those used for a Ford sedan or even an expensive Porsche or Lamborghini.

Street rod owners are different, too. They are more highly motivated to keep their cars looking good and more involved in every aspect of their cars. This book attempts to provide the means to detail your street rod—assuming that you already have the motivation. This book also assumes (I hope correctly) that the street rod to be detailed is in better condition than the typical daily driver *before* the detailing begins. For instance, there is no discussion of rubbing compounds used to peel off thick layers of oxidized paint. The engine section hardly mentions some of the most commonly used—and strongest—engine cleaning solvents in the belief that most street rod engines never get that dirty.

In terms of soap or wax, the shelves of nearly any auto parts store are loaded with a wealth of soaps, cleansers, glazes, waxes, whitewall cleaners, and about a million other products designed to help you clean and detail your car. It's always hard to decide which products to mention in a how-to book, and in this case it was especially difficult.

The products mentioned in the text and photos are those that I found to be in general use with serious street rodders and/or professional detailers. This is by no means an exclusive list and does not mean that other similar products from other manufacturers are inferior. I included those products I saw the most often, thinking they could be a starting point for the street rodder looking for the right materials to detail his or her rod.

In fact, after writing this book and asking a lot of questions, I believe there really are no "bad" products. Nearly all the products on the shelf carry brand names, and most will do what the labels claim. Because each street rod is a little different from the next and because different products are available in different parts of the country, each street rodder will have to do a little experimenting to find the products that work best for a particular car.

Leather interior requires different cleaners than does vinyl. Chrome wheels or accessories need different polish than do brushed aluminum wheels and parts. It's up to the car owner to find the right cleaners based on the guidelines presented here and his or her own experience.

In almost any endeavor, the difference between a good job and a sloppy one is in the little things. It sounds trite, but nowhere is that more true than in detailing a car. What I learned in writing this book is that anyone can wash a car, almost anyone can detail a car, but to do a really good detailing job requires a certain attitude. Yes, you might say it requires a certain fanatical attention to detail.

Chapter 1

The Street Rod Body

Washing your car might seem to be the simplest thing in the world. All it takes is a little soap, some water, and some elbow grease. Nothing to it, right?

Wrong.

Wrong, because we aren't just washing the car. We are thoroughly cleaning the vehicle, removing all possible dirt and debris from the paint, glass, and trim. We are cleaning the car, usually in preparation for other operations—such as polishing and waxing.

Wax should be applied to a clean car, and protectants must be applied to clean vinyl or rubber. A good wash job is the foundation for the entire detailing process.

The Wash Area

You can't overhaul an engine without access to a shop and the correct tools. Likewise, doing a high-quality wash job requires an area of your driveway or

The essentials of a good wash job: a long hose with a nozzle on the end, a big bucket, and plenty of terry cloth towels. The nice Deuce belongs to Steve Anderson.

Normally a wash in the sun is a no-no. But this is October in Minnesota, and the sun is anything but too hot. Note that the hose is long enough to reach around the car.

You need a nozzle that allows you to shut the water on and off. Use one that adjusts to a soft mist so it doesn't force water past the window and door seals. The nozzle also helps save water.

garage that can be set aside, if only temporarily, for the task. First, you need an area with access to water and a drain. If you're working outside, part of the driveway will work fine. Good drainage makes things easier and neater for the person doing the washing.

You need enough hose to reach all the way around the car. A hose that is too short will have you accidentally running the hose over the fender of the car to reach the car's far corners and inadvertently scratching the paint. The hose should be equipped with a nozzle of some kind to minimize the mess and conserve water.

Some detailers advocate the use of warm or hot water, claiming that it reduces water spots. This seems at best like an unnecessary expense and at worst like an outright waste. A better way to reduce spotting is by using soft water (in areas where the natural water is hard). Soft water reduces the mineral content of the water, thereby reducing water spots and allowing the soap to work more effectively as well.

Probably the best single way to reduce those unsightly spots is to never, never, never wash the car in the hot sun. When you spray water on a hot, black

After a good rinse to remove as much loose dirt and dust as possible, Eric Aurand starts washing the Deuce with a terry cloth towel and a mild soap solution.

hood, it evaporates in about two minutes. When the water is gone the only thing left behind is the minerals. The same minerals that form those nasty and hard-to-remove water spots.

Tools and Materials

If your garage looks anything like mine, finding the tools you want isn't always an easy job. The first thing you need is an old milk crate or bucket or box in which you can put everything. That way, if you only have twenty minutes to wash off the car, you won't spend those twenty minutes looking for the soap and brushes.

Before putting the correct soap in the water bucket, take off your rings, your watch, and most important of all, your belt. You don't do this because you might get the watch wet, but because the watch or the belt buckle will put nasty scratches in that fine Guard's-Red paint job.

Soap is another of those subjects that should be simple but isn't. Millions of street rodders probably wash their cars with dishwashing detergents. Yet, every professional detailer or painter warns that dishwashing detergent is too harsh and strips oils

Eric moves around the car, washing and rinsing a small section before moving on to another part of the car. Water spots are avoided by never allowing the soap and water solution—or even the rinse water—to evaporate off the car.

After rinsing the front fender, Eric does an initial wash of the inner fender panels. The inner fender panels and chassis will be detailed in full later.

After the wash job the entire car is wiped down with more terry cloth towels.

from the paint. So instead of dishwashing detergent, use a good car-washing soap.

The actual washing should be done with a wash mitt or soft cotton cloth rather than a sponge. The trouble with using a sponge is the tendency of the sponge to hold dirt and grit, thereby scratching the car as you move the sponge over the body surface. Buy a wash mitt made of cotton or wool if possible. These natural fibers are softer than synthetics and less likely to leave tiny scratches behind. Wash mitts should be washed on a regular basis (use a little fabric softener, too) to keep them clean and free of any dirt or sand.

The pro-street linkage is washed at this time, too, and will be polished and detailed later.

Of course you'll never use the mitt to wash the lower edges of the rocker panels or fender lips or the underside of fenders—or any area where the mitt is likely to pick up grit that will later scratch the finish. For those lower, grittier areas, you need a second mitt, a large sponge, or a brush. A number of brushes ranging in size from tiny to medium will aid the wash job. Toothbrushes are really unequaled for getting into small nooks, crannies, and seams along the edge of the trim. A 2in paint brush with soft bristles is a great tool for getting into grille work and seams. A larger brush—or two—with stiffer bristles will work well for tires and the underside of fenders.

On the end of the water hose, you need a nozzle. Most nozzles will allow you to turn the water on and off (saving a lot of water in the process) and adjust the spray pattern from a mist to a jet. Because some street rods don't seal real well where windows meet doors, it's best to have a nozzle that yields a gentle steam of water. That way there won't be so much water inside the car when the wash job is finished.

Some street rodders prefer to wash the car in the garage. In this case there may not be a drain, and even if there is, you probably don't want a great deal of water flying around the shop. The answer is a second bucket and an additional wash mitt or towel. The idea is to use one bucket for wash water, and one for rinsing. Likewise, you'll want one mitt for plain water and one for soapy water.

When you're all through with the wash and rinse, you need to dry the car. This is best done with a series of soft, clean, cotton towels, or cloth diapers.

Again, a chamois acts like a sponge and tends to pick up dirt and drag it across the paint all over the car.

The Wash Job

Before going after that Ford or Chevy with a soapy mitt, be sure the car is cool (not cool as in Elvis but cool as in chilly). It's always a good idea to start the wash job by rinsing off the car to remove as much dust and dirt as possible and eliminate the chance of picking up that material in the mitt and dragging it across the hood or fender.

Once you start, wash the car in small sections. Wet, wash, and rinse each section before going on to the next. That way the soap and water never have a chance to dry on the car (causing more of those dreaded water spots). It also keeps you focused and better able to really clean that small area before moving on to another one.

Always work from top to bottom, from high to low. This keeps grit flowing off the car and away from your mitt. As you work over an area, watch for the cracks, crevices, and grilles that can't be cleaned with the mitt. Take the toothbrush or paintbrush and work your soapy water into these areas as well. When one area is finished, rinse it thoroughly and move on to the next area. The idea is to keep the car wet throughout the washing process.

After washing the entire car, take the sponge or mitt saved for the really dirty areas and wash the inner fenders, fender lips, and the bottom of the rocker panels and splash pans.

Drying the car is probably best done in two steps. First, get most of the water off the car with your terry towels or cotton diapers. Then, go back over the car with a new set of towels and get off all the water. Any water spots that show up can be removed with a little cleaner or cleaner/wax (more on this later). Spots on the glass can be removed with a cleaner or polish.

After drying the car, you need to open the doors and wash or wipe the doorjamb area. If it isn't too dirty, a little soapy water on a terry towel is probably

Following the wash job the true detailing can begin—inside the shop with the car on ramps to make chassis detailing easier.

If you keep everything in a neat kit like this, it's a lot easier to find your supplies on wash day. A milk carton container works well, too.

These are some of the products Eric used to detail the exterior of the Deuce. Both Meguiar's and The Wax Shop make a variety of products for detailing both the inside and outside of your rod.

sufficient, followed by a dry towel. If the area has been left dirty for too long, it may require a thorough cleaning with a sponge or towel and some cleaning solution like Simple Green. If there is a road film with an oily consistency, a bucket of hot water will help to cut the film. Don't forget the lips of the hood and trunk at this time as well. The paintbrush and toothbrush are effective tools here, making it easier to get at all the little nooks and crannies.

When you think it's probably time to move on to the wheels and tires (or maybe go out for a cold beer), it's actually time to take the Q-tips out of the box and take a complete trip around the car. Use these to clean the heads of screws, the lip around rearview mirrors, the edges where trim meets a body panel, and the seams where two panels meet.

When you absolutely can't find any more dirt on the outside of the car—then it's time to move on to the next step.

The Post-Wash Dilemma
OK, the car is as clean as you can get it. It sparkles even in the most minute crevices. The dilemma is simple: What should you do now? The options are almost too numerous to count. If you go to the local parts store for help, the confusion only gets worse. The shelves are loaded with an amazing array of products, such as polishing and rubbing compounds, polish, cleaners, glaze, swirl removers, waxes, and cleaner/wax combinations.

Before going any further, we need to back up and start with some definitions. Just what is a wax? A cleaner? A glaze? And what is the difference between polishing compound and polish?

Definitions: Waxing Poetic on Sealers and Swirl Removers
In the old days, an oxidized paint job would be buffed out with buffing or polishing compound to restore the shine. The abrasives in the compound would polish off the top layers of oxidized paint, revealing a fresh and shiny layer underneath. Often a less abrasive material was used to take out the scratches left by the compound before the paint job was considered saved and ready for a good coat of wax.

Because street rods addressed in this book get maintenance that is better than average, the very abrasive polishing and buffing compounds have been left out. The cleaning and polishing products covered here start with the strongest and go to the mildest. It is assumed that no self-respecting rodder would allow his paint to go so far downhill that the very heavy abrasives contained in these compounds would be necessary.

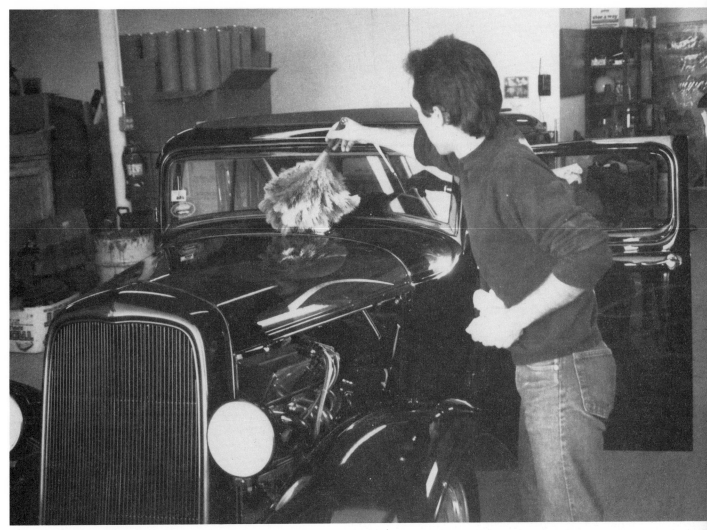

Before starting on the cleaning/waxing, Eric dusts the car to ensure there is no grit or dust on the surface.

By the way, readers should understand that there is no connection between the very abrasive polishing compounds and the polish (a rather mild product that might not even contain abrasives) discussed in this section. Readers also have to understand that the products used on a particular paint job depend on the type of paint. In particular, clear coats and candy jobs (especially in lacquer) must be handled with care so the top layers aren't stripped off. Clear coats protect the base coat and add to the shine. In most cases, once the clear coat is stripped off, the paint underneath weathers very quickly. In the case of a candy job, the color of the paint will be affected if too much of the top layers is removed.

Cleaners and Deoxidizers

Paint cleaners are designed to remove any dirt left after washing and to strip off any oxidized or "dead" paint. They range from products that contain

The paint on Steve's Deuce is in great shape so a cleaner/ polish is used only on selected areas such as the running boards.

13

abrasives to those that do all or most of their cleaning through chemical action. Those that contain little or no abrasives are often labeled "safe for clear-coat paint jobs." Cleaners that contain abrasives will be labeled as unsafe for clear-coat, or for use on "conventional" paint jobs.

There is much controversy regarding the durability of clear-coat paints and how easily a clear coat can be rubbed through during paint cleaning and polishing. Everyone associated with detailing or painting has an opinion.

Jon Kosmoski, owner of House of Kolor and a long-time manufacturer of custom paints, had this to say: "Most of today's custom paints are either lacquer or urethane. If you have a clear coat on the car, you need to know which type of paint it is. Generally one coat of urethane is up to twice as thick as one coat of lacquer. Urethanes are more flexible, and just plain tougher, than a lacquer paint job.

"I wouldn't say it's impossible to rub through a urethane clear coat. But if it's a good, catalyzed urethane clear coat, you would have to work pretty

Remember the Basics

In any endeavor, there are differences of opinion. Ask any three motorheads which is the best cam for a small-block Chevy and you're likely to get four answers. The same is true of detailing.

Whether it is the type of soap or the use of a chamois, people hold wildly divergent opinions. The only thing that anyone knows for sure is the fact that *their* way of washing, drying, or waxing is the *right one*!

In order to find some good answers, if not the right ones, I turned to Scott Lindsey, part owner of S&R Detailing (formerly Steve's) in Richfield, Minnesota. Scott has been detailing cars professionally for over six years, and has worked on everything from your basic Ford sedan to a Ferrari Testarossa. Scott offered to answer what are probably the most commonly asked questions about detailing.

What kind of soap is best to use on the car's body?

I know people use everything from dish soap to special, car-wash soap. People should not use dishwashing soap, the reason being that these are actually detergents, and they will strip any wax off the car. Instead, they should use soap meant for car washing, one of the good brand names. This will not strip the wax, and it will add oils to the paint instead of stripping oils from the paint.

The washing itself should not be done with a chamois or a sponge because they will retain dirt, maybe from the lower part of the car or rocker panels, and drag that dirt around and maybe scratch the paint. I like to use a mitt or a cotton terry towel. The mitts come in synthetic and natural fibers. They both seem to work fine.

What about polish, glaze, and cleaners? What's the difference between them, and when should one of the other be used?

Right now we're using more glazes than anything else. Most glazes don't have any abrasives or cleaners. There are lots of new, high-tech, and clear-coat paint jobs. You have to be real careful with them. Some of the paints are softer than others. With clear-coated paints you want to stay away from anything with a cleaner in it. That clear coat on new cars is usually pretty thin, and you don't want to rub through that clear coat.

(Author's note: See Jon Kosmoski's comments on clear coats in the body chapter.)

Instead of a cleaner, glazes, followed by polish or wax, usually suffice. Again, I usually apply these with soft terry towels.

If the car has good paint, without a lot of scratches, I would probably just hand wax it. If it's fairly scratchy, I might want to buff it with a machine to remove the scratches. We might go through two or more steps with the buffer. My rule of thumb is to start light and go heavier. So I would start with some glaze and only go to a cleaner or true compound if I absolutely had to—maybe in an area with a lot of oxidation or scratches.

I'm using more and more glazes. I put them between a cleaner and a polish. Less abrasive than a cleaner, the glazes really work well on the modern paint. They remove swirls and actually seem to fill the tiny scratches.

In a scratched area, you can use a cleaner and then a glaze. After putting on the glaze—like Meguiar's number seven—I work real hard to get it off. It can be kind of hard to get off. You can use something like this as a one-shot following the wash, or you can follow it up with a good coat of wax.

If you were going to follow the glaze with another protective step, what would it be, and what would you use?

If I were going to do a two-step process, I would use a good carnauba paste wax. Carnauba is the best. It's better than one of the newer polysealer products. Use a paste wax because it leaves less of a residue than the liquid. I use a Meguiar's carnauba product on my own car, and it lasts about four to six months. Of course, I only use car-wash soap to wash it, and I'm pretty careful with it. I'm a big believer in wax. I believe that if you take care of the paint, it will take care of you. Treat it nice, and it will last a lot longer.

Should amateurs use a buffer to buff the paint?

I say no. It's so easy to burn the paint or catch edges, or maybe even burn through the paint. People at home should probably work strictly by hand.

What about washing the wheels and tires? There is a bewildering array of products out there, so what should a person look for?

Yes, there are tons of different products out there. For wheels you have to be careful what you use. Some of them are too harsh and they can actually take the color out of a mag-type wheel, or in some cases, if the aluminum is porous, they can stain hard with a fairly abrasive product to rub through the clear coat layer. Regardless of which type of paint it is, we always recommend that you never cross an opening or go over a peak with your buffer or polishing towel. Even if you're working by hand, you should never concentrate on the peak or edge itself. It's kind of like a woman's high heel sinking into an asphalt parking lot. It isn't the weight, it's just that all the weight is concentrated on a very small area. When you run on an edge or peak, the effect is the same: modest pressure with a towel is concentrated

at that edge. When you are polishing, you should approach the peak or ridge from either side and stay away from the peak itself.

"The cleaners and polishes I like best are those with little or no abrasives, products that do their cleaning chemically. You can test the abrasiveness of a product by putting some on your fingernail and rubbing that nail with another fingernail. If it feels real gritty, find another product.

"When we rub a paint job by hand, we buy professional cotton polishing cloths. You can proba-

---

the aluminum itself. Eagle One makes some good products, with different products for different types of wheels. People should read the labels and ask the salesperson for advice before grabbing a wheel cleaner off the shelf. Simple soap and water will often work, with little chance of damaging an expensive wheel.

For washing tires, you can often use a simple cleaner, something like Simple Green. If they're real dirty or you have white walls, then there are special soaps at the parts store. Westley's Bleche-wite is good on whitewalls. Ajax or a bathroom-type cleaner works well, too.

For a dressing, you need a product that breathes. There are lots of products on the shelves. People should try to use a petroleum-based product rather than a water-based product. Some guys even use a little fresh oil to give the tires that "new" look.

What about interiors? Are there any tricks you've learned over the years?

Interiors are hard, partly because there are so many different materials used and partly because they do get pretty dirty and need a lot of attention. For leather seats, we've had good luck with the Lexol products. I see so many cars here in Minnesota with big cracks in the leather, cracks caused by no maintenance in a harsh climate. You need to keep them clean and then be sure to use a good leather conditioner that puts some oils back into the leather. If I were using a new product on my leather seats, I would try it first on the side of the seat to make sure it isn't going to pull the color out of the leather or harm it in any way.

For vinyl seats and interior, I use some of the same stuff I use on leather. The Lexol works well, and general cleaners—as long as they aren't mixed too strong—will usually work on vinyl.

For cloth upholstery, many shampoos and cleaners are available. They all seem to work pretty well. When we have a real dirty carpet or pair of seats, we get an extractor, like a "Rug-Doctor," because this will actually pull the dirt out of the material. Sometimes you can wash the material and then go over it with a wet-and-dry vacuum to pull dirt from the fabric.

What are the mistakes that people most commonly make when they detail their cars?

They wash the car in the sun, when the metal is hot, and they use dishwashing detergent. In the hot

sun like that, the detergent action is increased. It's hard on the paint, it tends to leave water spots that are hard to remove, and it's probably the single biggest mistake people can make. Water spots can be real, real hard to remove—sometimes you can't even get them out by machine. The best idea is to avoid them in the first place.

The other mistake people make is to forget the basics. Detailing is a nook-and-cranny business. You've got to look high and low for the dirt. You have to use a toothbrush and some Q-tips and really get in there with some elbow grease. There is no magic wand or silver bullet, just hard work and attention to detail.

Scott Lindsey of S&R Detailing in Richfield, Minnesota, has been doing professional detailing for more than six years. Scott feels you should always start with the mildest product in any situation and proceed to a stronger one only when the mild one won't do the job.

Smooth running boards always seem to catch hell, no matter how careful the owner is. Scratches like these *probably can be eliminated with a good polish and plenty of elbow grease.*

Following the use of the cleaner/polish, the wax is applied. Though it's called a glaze, this product from The Wax Shop is actually a liquid wax. Be sure to read the labels on any detailing products you buy so you know what you are getting.

bly get them at any paint supply house. Some of the cloths have a real tight weave and don't really let the polish work correctly. There is also the chance that they might put very small scratches in the paint. The professional cloths have a real open weave, they're real soft, and they do a great job."

Unless your rod has somehow developed badly weathered paint, you probably don't need the abrasives, no matter what kind of paint you have. To quote Scott Lindsey of S&R Detailing in Minneapolis: "When in doubt as to which product to use on any job, I always recommend that you start with the mildest and then proceed to a stronger product only if the mild product isn't doing the job."

In the case of cleaners for the paint, also start with one that contains little or no abrasive (even if it's not a clear-coat paint job) and proceed to a stronger product only if the original choice isn't doing the job.

Most professional shops use a buffer of some type for their cleaning and polishing. Even some books aimed at the non-professional detailer recommend the use of a buffer. This book recommends otherwise. Buffers, especially the commercial or high-speed models, run as high as 2600rpm. In the hands of a novice, that much speed and power can quickly cut through or burn the paint.

Better suited to the individual working at home are the smaller orbital buffers. These run at about 1600rpm and are designed to minimize the odds on burning or cutting through the paint. Even these, however, can do more harm than good. The recommendation here is to clean and detail your rod by

Dick Cox is the owner of this nice '34 Ford. He washes the car in the shop—with no floor drain. He uses plain water and a sponge for the washing, working one small area at a time. After washing, each area is wiped dry with a cotton diaper.

Following the wash job, Dick likes to clean the windows with a glass cleaner. A variety of glass cleaners and glass polish are available for detailing your street rod.

After washing and drying the car, Dick goes over the whole thing with Meguiar's number seven, a good polish/cleaner.

hand. You will be able to do just as good a job (maybe better) than an individual working with a machine. It will just take a little longer.

Paint Polish or Glaze

These products come under a variety of names, including polish, glaze, and swirl remover. Even after going over a good paint job with a cleaner, there are usually some tiny scratches and imperfections left behind. Rather than apply the wax over these little scratches or spider webbing, the polish-type products will let you further smooth the finish.

The glaze products contain more than just fine polishing agents, they contain resins that actually fill some of those tiny scratches in the paint (thus the "swirl remover" label). Some professional shops use a two-step polishing process, using a polish first, followed by a glaze. The better glaze products provide more depth to the paint (like a good lacquer job or clear coat), and give the paint a nice wet look. In some cases, a glaze is the only way to remove the smallest of those imperfections in the paint.

A toothbrush or small brush like the one shown here is a great tool for cleaning wax residue from around lights and trim.

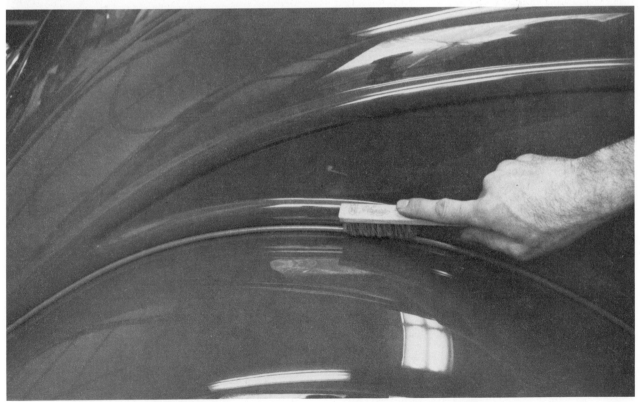

The body welting also will need to be cleansed of any wax and polish build-up. By masking off these areas, or being very careful in the wax application, you can eliminate much of the need for this cleanup.

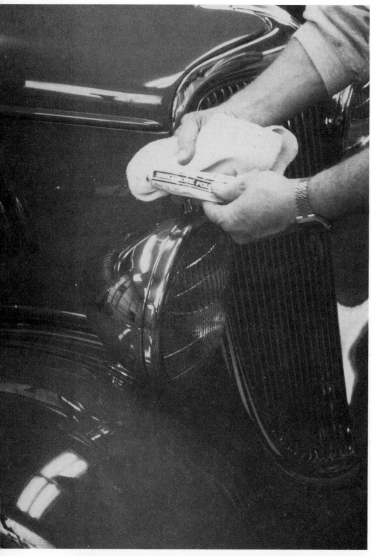

The thing you learn in detailing is that the things you thought were clean really aren't. This stainless light housing looked OK until Dick started in on it with Semi-chrome polish, his favorite for stainless steel.

A little work with the polish and a soft towel and soon the towel is covered with the dark oxidation that had been coating the light housing.

Wax

A good wax will provide protection for the paint while adding shine to the finish. Though there are a variety of new polysealants on the market, most professionals prefer to work with good, old-fashioned carnauba wax. They note that paint needs to be protected but it also needs to breathe. A good wax will do just that, a sealer probably won't. Some professionals feel the sealers actually last too long and allow oxidation to build up under the sealer.

All the best waxes claim to be a carnauba wax. You may be wondering: what the heck is carnauba? Carnauba is a nut from a Brazilian palm tree (known in Latin as *Copernica cerifera*), a tree found in only two of Brazil's provinces. The oil from the nut is the source of the magical carnauba wax. A good car-

nauba wax has the advantage of protecting the paint while allowing it to breathe at the same time. Carnauba is said to be the hardest of the many oils used to manufacture waxes. A purist will settle for nothing less than high-quality carnauba wax in paste form. Keep in mind, however, that even the best wax will only last four to six months before another application is needed.

Combination Products

Americans love convenience, and the manufacturers of cleaning and paint-care products have responded with a variety of products that claim to do two or even three jobs at once. Many of the waxes on the shelf contain various cleaning agents. While the results will seldom match the job done by separate products, some of these time savers work well when you have to leave for the show in twenty minutes. Among the most commonly used combination products are the cleaner-waxes manufactured by all the major companies. These products should be checked for abrasive content but are otherwise a great aid when there just isn't time for a full three-

The "after" photo. Without the oxidation, and polished to a high luster, the stainless housing shines as it should. Each part of the car needs to get this kind of attention.

step detailing job. Cleaner-waxes also work well on a variety of polished and chrome surfaces, with just enough cleaner to strip off any oxidation while leaving a nice layer of wax behind to protect the finish.

Detailing the Body

After the car wash, it's time to detail the paint job on your street rod. Even though the paint may be in great shape, you probably need to start with a cleaner to remove the inevitable oxidized layer of paint.

The cleaner should be a mild product with little or no abrasives; a product compatible with your paint. You need a clean cotton cloth or terry towel, folded so it fits comfortably in the palm of your hand. Apply the cleaner to the cloth (not directly to the paint), and work the cleaner into the paint in an area of no more than about three or four square feet. It's best to work on one small area at a time. As you work, the cloth will pick up paint and need to be turned over frequently. As the cleaner is wiped off the paint, the paint's shine will improve.

As you work across the car, be careful at edges and creases (if the cleaner you're using contains *any* abrasives), because you can rub through one layer of paint even when you're working by hand. After

The consensus is in—use car-wash soap for cleaning the car, not dishwashing detergent. This shampoo is a new product from the busy boys at Boyd's.

There are more car care and detailing products on the shelf at the parts store than any one person can use. Think *about the product you really need and then be sure to read the label before taking anything home.*

completely cleaning the entire car, take a minute to carefully and slowly walk around the car. Look for any areas that look rougher than the rest and go over these with a little more cleaner.

After the cleaning operation, you need to follow the same basic procedure with the polish of your choice. Apply the polish to a clean, folded towel and work it into the paint. Manufacturers have slightly different notions about whether the polish should be allowed to dry or be kept wet during the polishing process, so follow the specific recommendations on the can or bottle. You need to work one small area at a time before moving on.

Though the paint may look great at this point, the purest of the pure will insist on one more step before applying any wax. Even though the paint is clean and flat, before applying wax you will want to fill small scratches and create the wet look.

Most polishes and nearly all the products labeled as a glaze contain resins that will soak into the paint. These resins fill the scratches and create the wet look. You need to apply a second layer of the polish, or a finishing glaze, and allow it to sit on the car for ten minutes before wiping it off. This sitting

Wash mitts are available in a variety of fabrics and styles. Professionals prefer the mitts because they hold plenty of water and don't trap grit between the mitt and the paint where it might cause a scratch in the paint.

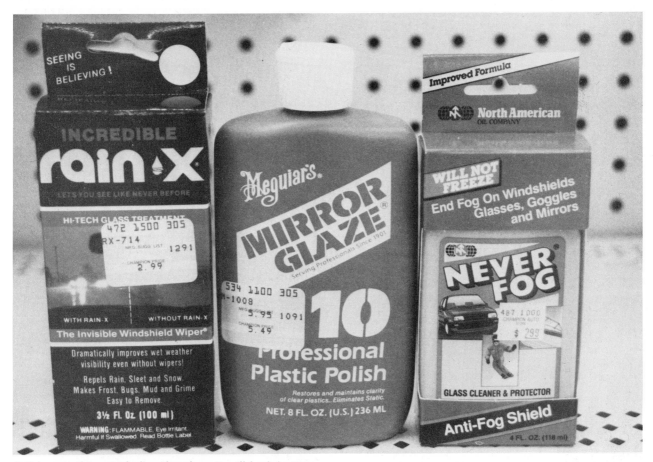

Polish everything, including the glass. It will look better, and water will run off like magic. Most automotive glass cleaners include some very fine polish.

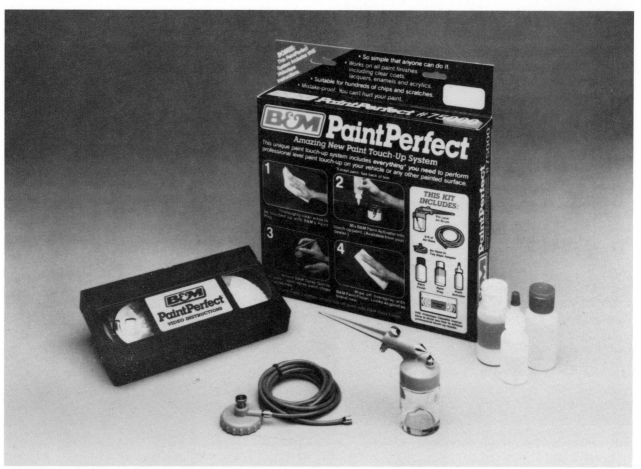

B&M has a neat touch-up kit available for repair of small scratches and chips in the paint. The kit includes an air brush and B&M's own Prep, Activator, and Finish. The only thing you supply is the touch-up paint and a modest amount of talent.

Companion to their PaintPerfect kit, B&M also offers the PolishPerfect kit. The kit includes their own polish—which can be safely applied in the sun—and a videotape of detailing tips as demonstrated by "well-known automotive model, K.C. Winkler."

time will allow the resins to actually soak into the paint, creating the effect you want.

Now—finally—you can put on a good layer of the genuine carnauba wax. As the instructions say, rub the wax into the paint with a circular motion. The circular motion works the wax into the paint, causing the wax to melt at the paint surface. More wax at this point is not necessarily better. Two light coats work better than one heavy coat in terms of shine and protection.

Though the instructions on the can always advise you to let the wax dry or cloud over before removal, one professional street rod detailer feels otherwise. Far-Out Gary from Los Angeles wipes off the wax right away. He insists that the longer the wax dries, the harder it is to wipe off, and the harder you wipe, the more likely it is that you will put tiny scratches in the paint. If you want the added protection of multiple coats of wax, allow the first coat to cure for a week before applying the second.

Always work one small area at a time. Apply, wipe off, and buff a fender before moving on to the door or running board. The problem with the wax is

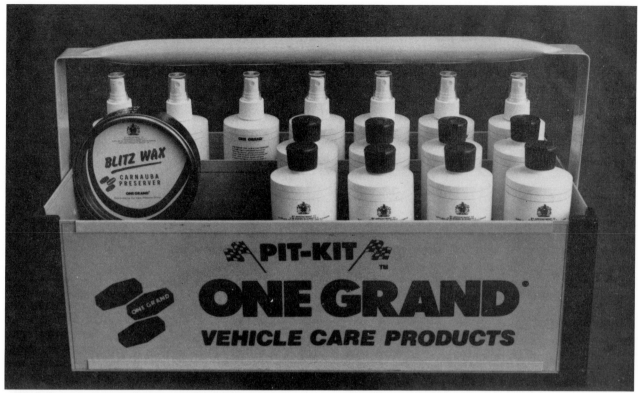

One Grand Company offers a complete line of car care products including their well-respected Blitz Wax. They also offer a complete mini kit of their detailing products for the first-time user.

Among their other products, One Grand offers a very good product catalog and technical guide filled with useful information for the automotive enthusiast.

Better known for their mag wheel polish, the folks at Mothers offer a full line of products, including this carnauba paste wax. Yes, carnauba wax really does seem to be the very best wax for an automobile. Note the label states, "No cleaners."

The Meguiar's line includes a polish, glaze, or wax for nearly any need. This is their professional line, available in many auto parts stores and used by street rodders and professional detailers alike.

its tendency to accumulate in the little crevices and cracks—places you don't want it. Nothing makes a car look worse than the telltale white seams and edges where the wax has built up and was never removed.

You can avoid some of that sloppy look by waxing very lightly at the edges. Some people tape off the edges and seams with thin masking tape. If the inevitable buildup still occurs, you will just have to deal with it when the rest of the job is done. When the wax job is finally finished and the paint glows with that hand rubbed look, you still have one more job to do.

The tools for this operation are a toothbrush and maybe a paintbrush with the bristles taped for most of their length. (This creates a soft bristle brush that is still fairly stiff.) Walk slowly around the car and use the brushes to carefully clean the white wax accu-

mulation from the edges of the trim, the taillights, and door handles (if you've still got door handles). Your wax job isn't really finished until all the residue has been removed.

When you're finished with the washing, cleaning, and waxing, your rod should look great. All oxidation has been removed, small swirls and tiny scratches have been eliminated or filled, and the fresh coat of wax will help to keep it looking this way.

How often you perform this task depends on how much you use the car. A good wax job lasts from four to six months. So maybe twice a year is the correct interval for a full detailing. Since most rods sit inside at least part of the winter, the detailing might be done when the car comes out in the spring and once more in mid-season. Between the full detailing sessions, you can take a few shortcuts and use some ideas from the chapter on two-hour detailing.

When you're confident about the quality and protection of your wax and polish, a little rain won't even bother you— or your car. On show days when rain is a possibility, take *along some good drying cloths just in case.* Rodder's Digest

Chapter 2

Engine Detailing

Introduction

Street rod engines are different than the engine in your Chevy Blazer or Ford van. The engine in a hot rod or street rod is usually designed to be seen. Even if your car has hood sides, or if it's a fat-fendered rod, the hood is often up so people can see all that shining detail. Many serious rodders spend hours and hours grinding all the lumps off the engine block, then finishing it and painting it to match the rest of the car. When the engine is assembled, chrome, polished, and billet parts are bolted on in place of the stamped or cast parts from Detroit. The effect is a very bright engine and engine compartment, one that was created with abundant TLC, and one that will take extra TLC to detail and keep looking bright and fresh.

If the engine is dirty and you intend to use a strong solvent for cleaning, it's important to keep that strong stuff off the fenders and other body parts. Use caution along with some kind of fender covers to protect the paint.

Because the engine is usually the dirtiest part of the car, many owners wash the engine first. This way, any overspray or grime that gets onto the fenders will be cleaned off during the wash job that follows. The order of washing really depends on how dirty everything is and your own personal preference. More important, however, is consistency. Find a sequence of wash operations that makes sense for you and your car, and stick with it so you achieve the same great job every time.

Wash That Small-Block

The trouble with washing a street rod or hot rod engine is that the products designed to wash engines or detail under the hood are often too harsh for serious street rod detailing. Gunk and other solvent-based products, so common on the shelf of your auto parts store, are far too strong for that engine block painted Ford Truck Yellow just like the body on your '34 Ford.

Solvent-based products available off the shelf will strip the grease and oil film off the engine (if your engine is that dirty). They may also remove a

The small-block in Doug's Graffiti coupe is essentially clean. Detailing an engine like this is a matter of touching up any chipped paint and polishing the abundant chrome. Pictured are two of the many good polishing products that might be used.

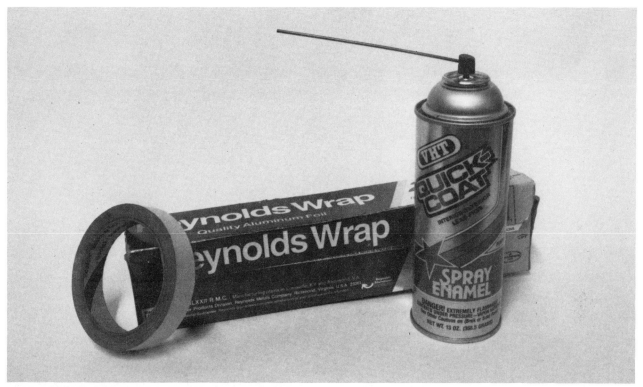

Tools for engine detailing: masking tape, aluminum foil (useful for masking off small areas and odd shapes), and a can of touch-up paint.

certain amount of paint. Even if they don't strip off the paint, they often bleach the color from the paint, so your block will no longer be Ford Truck Yellow but something much lighter. If the engine in your rod is really dirty and oily, you may have no choice. If you use a strong cleaner, just don't leave it on for a long time in order to minimize the chance it will bleach your engine paint.

The high-pressure spray at the self-serve car wash is another great engine cleaning aid—if it's the grungy engine on your tow car. The high-pressure spray *will* blast off all that dirt and grime, but it will also blast off the paint. Individuals who have restored cars need to be especially careful since the high-pressure spray will also blow off the factory stickers and decals that were so hard to find.

If you can't use all those normal engine cleaning aids, what can you use to wash and detail your street rod engine? The answer is soap and water combined with elbow grease and common sense.

Though dishwashing detergent may be too harsh for the paint on your car, it works pretty well for washing the engine. Designed to cut grease, dish soap can be mixed as strong as you need and brushed onto the engine. If your engine is never very dirty, a diluted solution will suffice. If, however, you let things go too long, a stronger mixture will probably get the grime off those chrome valve covers and the body-color engine block.

Getting the paint where you want it is much easier if a spray nozzle with an extension tube is inserted in place of the regular spray nozzle. This nozzle was borrowed from a spray can of carb cleaner.

Aluminum foil will bend to nearly any shape and effectively mask off things like hoses and distributor caps. The *foil works much better than paper and masking tape and can be used again and again.*

The water in the bucket should be as hot as you can stand it. The difference in the grease-cutting ability of hot and cold water is something you have to see to appreciate. The use of rubber gloves will let you run the water nice and hot and avoid getting dreaded dishpan hands.

Apply the soap solution to the engine with a dedicated sponge or a paintbrush. Dirty areas can be worked over with the paintbrush or even a stiff-bristled parts-washing brush. As with the body, you will have better luck if you can keep the engine wet, washing a small area and rinsing it before moving on to another small area.

When you're finished washing, wipe down the engine with more terry towels. Compressed air (if available) can be used to get the water out of the little nooks and crannies. Q-tips are handy here as a

means of getting into those tight spots when cleaning and, later, when drying.

By avoiding the high-pressure wash syndrome, you eliminate most of the need to seal distributor caps and carburetors from all that water. You will have to be careful with the water hose, of course, but the low-pressure water from the garden hose is much easier to control than the high-pressure blast at the car wash. Small plastic bags and sandwich bags can be used to cover the distributor cap, carburetor, and breather. If you take the breather/fill cap out of the valve cover, a small piece of duct tape can be used to seal the valve cover during the wash.

Is Waxing the Engine Block a Better Idea?

The emphasis that rodders place on a good-looking engine has caused some to go to extreme

The engine in Steve's Deuce is filled with plenty of polished and chrome-plated goodies—all calling for a bit of polish or cleanser.

lengths to ensure a good-looking engine. Beyond cleaning and polishing, some rodders have tried to make the engine block really shine through the application of wax. All indications show it *just don't work.* Unless you have finished the block to a mirror-smooth surface, the little lumps and bumps of the block won't allow you to really get in there to remove all the hazy wax and buff the surface after applying the wax. In return for a lot of extra work, the usual result is a block with hazy white areas where the wax couldn't be or wasn't buffed sufficiently.

What About the Chrome and Billet Goodies?

Once the engine is clean, you need to go over it piece by piece to make sure it looks as good as it possibly can. The products you use are going to depend on what kind of goodies you've got under the hood and how much dirt and grime are attached to those chrome goodies.

If your chrome air cleaners and valve covers are really dirty or oxidized, then a good chrome polish is the best product for the job. Chrome parts that are less tarnished can usually be cleaned up with a good cleaner/wax. The mild abrasive in most of these products will provide a nice shine, and the wax will help keep it looking that way until the next detail job. Those nice chrome headers can be cleaned best with chrome polish as well. Try not to leave any residue on the headers, or the heat will often turn it into a stain that can be difficult to remove.

Billet goodies and aluminum should be cleaned with a product intended for brushed aluminum. Too much of the wrong polish used too often on the billet parts will eventually leave them pretty shiny—maybe not the finish you originally had in mind. A Scotch-Brite pad (available in two "grits") is a great way to clean aluminum and retain the brushed finish. You could also try polish intended for brushed aluminum wheels or the brushed parts under the

Eric gives the valve covers a wipe down with a cleaner/wax product.

The polished headers are wiped down with Windex (they weren't very dirty or oxidized), and soiled areas are polished anew.

hood. In general, a brushed aluminum surface needs a coarser polishing material than a polished or chrome surface. Be sure to read the far-out interview with Far-Out Gary for some great tips on engine detailing.

Some Special Products for Detailing Under the Hood

There are a number of special products made for detailing under the hood. The new Eastwood catalog carries four items that might be of particular interest to street rodders. Eastwood's Stainless Steel Coating is intended for exhaust manifolds and ex-haust systems and is said to keep them rust-free for long periods of time. To achieve just the right degree of gray for aluminum or steel parts under the hood, Eastwood also carries Spray Grey, Detail Grey, and Aluma Blast. While some of these are more easily applied when the parts are off the car, they seem ideally suited to the enthusiast who wants a perfect-looking engine compartment.

Tricks and Tips

Given the harsh under-hood environment, the paint on your engine is prone to fading and chipping, even with the greatest care. Some of that wear and

The engine in Dick's Ford carries a number of chrome-plated accessories. Here the exhaust manifold covers get a once-over with the polish and a clean towel.

While you're detailing the engine, don't forget the bottom. Polished oil pans and headers get a lot of abuse—road rash and tar combined with an oily film from the engine.

A very bright engine compartment in a Roger Ward-built custom. Detailing something like this is going to involve a number of different products—each designed to deal with a different material or finish—and a lot of work to clean all those louvers.

An engine like Jim Prokop's Mopar—left in mostly factory trim—is relatively easy to detail and requires only that you get it clean.

It's not really a Packard, but rather a small-block in a Doug Thompson-built Packard. The key here is making the chrome sparkle, and Richard obviously has done a good job of that.

35

No, not a lot of chrome here—you can throw away the Blue Magic. About all you can do is keep it clean.

tear can be avoided by using a high-quality paint during the initial painting. Specifically, catalyzed urethane from a company like PPG or House of Kolor is much, much more durable than a straight enamel or a lacquer. In most cases, common engine and body colors can be found at the local parts store, often in a high-temperature formula.

If, in spite of good materials and maintenance, the paint under the hood has taken a beating, there are some tricks to help get everything looking new again. Painting under the hood without a complete disassembly requires some special techniques. In order to avoid painting the polished headers when painting the block or intake manifold, some careful masking-off is needed.

Rather than fight with normal masking tape and paper, tin foil is a better idea. Just tear off a sheet and

mold it to cover the hose or alternator you need to protect from the new paint (be a little careful around the hot terminals as the foil will conduct electricity). It bends to nearly any shape and can be used over and over again.

For getting paint into really tight places, the paint can's spray nozzle should be swapped with a WD-40 type of nozzle—one with a long tube. This way you can spot in a little paint very precisely in the area where you need it.

Sometimes it's easier to touch up the paint with a small brush. After the wash job, the edges of the spark plugs may get a light coating of rust. Rather than replace the plug, just touch up the metal section with a small brush and a little black paint.

Anyone with anodized aluminum parts on the engine should be careful with the polishing material.

A relatively plain Jane and a good case for soap and water followed by some cleaner/wax.

The actual anodized color is usually only a few thousandths of an inch thick. Polish off too much metal and you polish off the color as well.

Finishing Up

Rubber parts and plug wires need to be wiped clean with something that will remove any oily film without attacking the rubber or neoprene material itself. If soap and water won't do the trick, mineral spirits can be relied on to do a nice job without causing any harm.

For the engine that isn't very dirty or the rodder in a big hurry to get on the road, there's always window cleaner. Yes, the light solvent action of a cleaner like Windex works well under the hood. It cuts through light dirt and oil film, softening everything so the parts can be wiped off with a terry towel or two. This is not detailing, but rather a "quick and dirty" engine wash for those times when time is tight.

The End Result

When you're all finished, the engine and the under-hood accessories will look the same as they did the day you pulled the car out of the garage for the first time. The chrome will sparkle, the billet will shine and the paint will look fresh and clean. The TLC spent in detailing the engine will bring back to life all the extra attention to detail that was used in assembling the engine in the first place.

A wax with a cleaner makes a good final step for chrome and polished parts under the hood. The cleaner helps to remove any oxidation, and the wax brings out a nice shine and protects the metal until the next detailing job is done.

If you're going to have your hood open, you had better make sure the engine and engine compartment have been detailed. If you've got an engine that looks as good as this, open it at every opportunity. Rodder's Digest

If you've got special equipment under your hood, it's going to draw extra attention, so pay extra attention to detailing your engine. People are going to be looking closely, so make sure they're impressed by what they see. Rodder's Digest

You may be able to open one side of your hood at a time, like this, but that doesn't mean you only need to detail one side of the engine. Assume that you might be asked to open the other side as well and detail everything. Rodder's Digest

This air cleaner cover is positioned so its grooves run parallel with those atop the valve covers, and the symmetry adds to the overall look. Keep this in mind when you look at things such as hose clamps that could be positioned in a uniform way. Rodder's Digest

Chapter 3

Chassis Detailing

Introduction

Just as the engine in your rod was designed—at least in part—for looks, the chassis and suspension components of most street rods are also designed and purchased with an eye toward their visual appeal. When you detail the car, detailing the chassis and all the various suspension components is very much a part of the operation. If you show your hot rod or street rod in the ISCA or local car show, even more emphasis is placed on a well-detailed chassis.

Tools and materials

For starters, you need soap—more of the stuff you used to wash the car and probably something stronger as well, such as dishwashing detergent and maybe some Simple Green or good all-purpose cleaner. You need a sponge or wash mitt dedicated to the bottom of the car—that way you won't drag any under-car grit across that nice paint job. A short bristle brush is very handy, too, as a means of scrubbing those extra-grubby frame and chassis areas.

Tar remover is handy here, as is a little Gunk or solvent-based cleaner. Don't use any gasoline, it's too dangerous. Make sure the cleaner/wax is at hand, along with some chrome polish and maybe a little touch-up paint in the color of the frame and inner

Cleaning and detailing the chassis is tough if the car is on the ground. Here the Deuce is up on ramps in front and on blocks in the rear. The higher the car, the better access you will have to everything underneath.

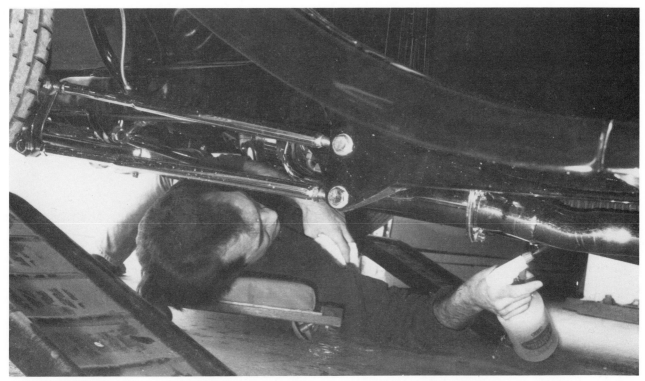

Eric uses Windex to clean polished chassis parts that aren't very dirty or oxidized. Each chassis part—chrome, pol- ished steel, and aluminum—needs a slightly different approach from the person doing the detailing.

A cleaner/wax is a good choice for chrome chassis parts if they aren't real dirty and don't require a lot of polishing. The cleaner/wax does clean the metal and also leaves a protective coating of wax. The same product works well on frame rails if they have a smooth finish.

There is no secret to good detailing. It's just a matter of getting in there and cleaning everything, even the exhaust system, until all the parts sparkle like new.

Eric leaves nothing to chance. After the exhaust system there's the rear-end housing and linkage to clean. This Deuce isn't very dirty, so Windex (or a similar cleaner) does a good job of cleaning the chrome and polished rear suspension linkage.

fenders. You also need a good jack and at least two jack stands or ramps.

Getting started

As low as most rods are, it's hard to get under there to do any cleaning unless the car is up on jack stands. Cleaning the tires and wheels is more easily done by removing the wheels. That means jacking up the car and taking off the wheels—a good starting point for the chassis detailing.

We've all heard it before, but, once again: don't crawl under the car, even for just a minute, unless the car is in fact supported by jack stands. Though it takes longer to get the car well up off the ground, you can do a much, much better job of cleaning and detailing the underside of the car when it's well up off the ground. When you jack up the car, use a shop towel between the jack and frame and another between the frame and jack stand to prevent chipping the paint on the frame. Once one or both ends are well up in the air, the chassis detailing can begin.

The Actual Detailing

Once the car is up in the air and the wheels are removed, start with the inner front fenders. A wash mitt or brush and a good, strong soap-and-water solution will clean off most of the road grime. Tar remover will take off anything the soap and water won't. Unless the underside of your fenders are finished to the same perfection as the outside of the car, you probably don't want to wax this surface.

When the inner fenders are clean, touch up any rock chips with more of the undercoat or flat black or body-color paint. Speaking of inner fenders, many street rodders are lining these with plastic liners to reduce the pounding that fenders on early rods take. The liners prevent dents and "stars" in the fender created by rocks thrown up by the tires.

With the wheels off the car, it's a good time to clean the front rotors and calipers. A wash with mild wheel cleaner should remove any brake dust on the rotors or drums, and a little touch-up paint will have them looking like new. The same applies to the calipers, first a cleaning, then a little touch-up paint or polish, depending on the finish. Don't forget to inspect the brake pads for wear while you're down there doing all that cleaning.

The soap and materials you use on the suspension components will depend on what they are made

If possible, pull off the wheels and clean each rotor and caliper separately. Here you can see the fine layer of brake dust that coats the front caliper.

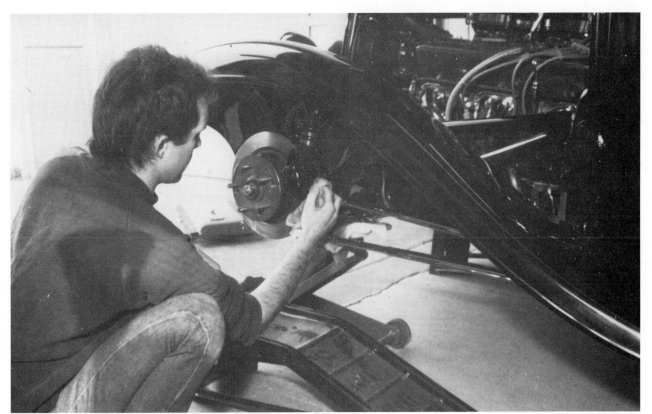

Cleaning the rotor and caliper starts with a soap-and-water solution or a general purpose-tire and wheel cleaner—something that will cut the road film and brake dust. Then *move in to further clean and detail each caliper and rotor with polish, touch-up paint, or whatever the job requires.*

43

Before: The dropped axle on Doug's Deuce is in need of a little TLC.

During: The backing plate, axle and shock are milky with polishing material (in this case Quator). Remember that all polishing materials are not created equal. Polishes meant for aluminum might not work and could scratch a chrome-plated surface.

of and how they are finished. Chrome A-frames need soap and water followed by polish or a cleaner/wax. Aluminum parts call for aluminum cleaner, maybe one intended for aluminum wheels, followed by polish or a Scotch-Brite pad. Stamped steel factory pieces will clean up with soap and water followed by touch-up paint.

While you're under the car, do a thorough visual inspection and check all components for wear. Be sure to look over the shocks because a small oil leak from a shock spreads a film of oil on everything nearby and makes a real mess.

A professional detailer once said that detailing is "a nook and cranny business." Nowhere is that statement more true than when you get to the chassis. The straight axle under a Deuce, with its leaf spring, shackles, bat-wings, and radius rods, is nothing if not a whole lot of nooks and crannies. Exposed

to the elements as chassis components are, those nooks and crannies are usually in serious need of cleaning.

Part of this job will require something stronger than car-wash soap, something that will cut an oily film. Access to these little areas being somewhat difficult, you might want to work on one small area at a time. After an initial cleaning you may need to go over the components with tar-and-grease remover. This solvent will strip off the tar picked up from the highway.

Once a component or group of components has received a general cleaning, you can start in with the smaller brushes and the toothbrush. Sometimes an old terry cloth towel can be worked into an area that's hard to reach, but if you're going to get these areas *really* clean, Q-tips will be needed.

The next step for polished or plated parts is the chrome polish, applied with a clean terry cloth, then buffed off per the instructions on the container. After washing the components, some street rodders just apply a cleaner/wax as a means of eliminating water spots. This can achieve a good shine and leave a protective coat of wax on everything.

If the frame rails are highly visible (on an early Ford, for example), you will probably want to be sure the area is more than just clean. Dry these visible frame and chassis areas much as you would the body. How far you go with the frame rails will depend on how far you (or the car's builder) went in finishing the rails. If they were block-sanded and painted to match the finish of the body, you may want to follow the same three-step detailing process you did for the body. If the rails are smooth, but not that smooth, a little cleaner/wax will leave a nice shine and eliminate any water spots. If they have a rough texture, you will have to settle for a good wash job.

After both front inner fenders have been cleaned, along with all the front suspension components, it's time to clean the bottom of the engine. Before going after it with the soap and water, look over everything for any telltale oil or water leaks. If

After: Polishing with the Quator and a soft towel make the axle and shock absorber shine like they should.

Jim Prokop's chassis is sophisticated; it's a combination of hand-built and Detroit suspension components. Detailing a suspension like this is a matter of soap and water followed by touch-up paint.

45

Whether or not you wax the frame rails depends on their finish. If they have been left a little rough, soap and water are about as far as you can go.

As the chassis in a street rod gets more sophisticated with more components and more polished and plated parts, the detailing gets to be a lot more work.

one lower corner of the engine is oily, take the time to trace the oil back to its source. Also take a peek at the back side of the water pump for any sign of leakage—nothing makes a nastier mess than a thin film of antifreeze on all those nice polished parts. If there are no leaks, just use a strong soap-and-water solution and some old rags.

If they aren't too dirty and oxidized, polished headers and stainless exhausts will clean up with a mild ammonia or alcohol-type cleaner. Some fine, chrome-type polish will restore any lost brilliance. Don't use anything that will leave a film on the exhaust system. If the exhaust system on your rod is stainless steel, you will want to detail all those pipes and mufflers too. If the exhaust is dirty, a light solvent should remove most of the dirt. The next step is polishing with a good stainless polish on a terry towel.

At the rear of the car, the procedure pretty much follows that used at the front. Clean the inner fenders, then the brake drums or rotors. A little touch-up paint or polish will have all the parts looking good as new.

If yours is an independent rear suspension, then there is a lot of painstaking cleaning to do. Each axle and U-joint needs to be cleaned with something strong enough to remove the road grime and oily film—and then polished to a nice luster. Some rodders use a strong solvent-based cleanser, but you might want to try something milder (like dishwashing detergent) first. When you grease all those U-joints, be sure to carefully wipe off any extra grease, or you'll be detailing it all over again soon. Also watch for any leaks from the center section and the wheel hubs.

Cleaning the drive shaft and the polished axles in your Boyd independent suspension requires more of the same attention to detail. Having the car on jack stands really helps here because with the car off the ground, you can rotate the drive shaft and half-shafts to get everything clean. A terry cloth works well to clean the U-joints; just coat it with a little bug-and-tar remover or solvent, pass it through the joint, and then work it back and forth. A terry towel and the cleaner of your choice work well on coil-wound shocks, too. The toothbrush is helpful in getting all those rear suspension and driveline goodies looking good as new again.

No Matter How Low . . .

A person would think that with all the street rods getting lower and lower no one would take the time to get down on their hands and knees to look underneath at suspension components and such. If that were the case, the owner of a really low car could skip most of the chassis detailing chores.

Yet, a strange kind of logic seems to prevail here. As a street rodder friend noted recently: "It's weird. It seems like the lower the car is, the more people want to get down and look underneath. Maybe they're trying to figure out how you got it so low."

So no matter how low you've got your ride, no matter how deep into the weeds it sits, other rodders are still going to crawl on their bellies to have a peek at the glories and secrets hiding underneath. You've got no choice but to get it clean, clean, clean.

The polished components on a front suspension like this Boyd-built suspension will need more than soap and water. A situation like this calls for an extra thorough washing followed by aluminum polish and wax for the perfectly finished frame rails.

There are a lot of components here. Far-Out Gary uses Gunk when a system like this gets good and dirty. Tar remover would work well, too, followed by polish or cleaner/wax.

Remember, the sexier your ride, the more likely it is that people will crawl on their bellies to look at the bottom side. If you get to polishing a suspension like this, remember that some of the components are polished aluminum, and some are steel.

The new wheel polish from Boyd's would work equally well on most polished aluminum parts, including chassis parts. This product is in the middle of the pack in terms of its abrasiveness. It contains ammonia to aid cleaning and wax to leave a protective coating on the parts.

Chapter 4

Wheels and Tires

Introduction

Anyone who doubts the importance of the wheels and tires in the overall construction of a modern hot rod or street rod hasn't looked at what a nice set of Boyd's wheels and radial tires costs these days. Whether your car is equipped with the latest billet wonders or factory steel wheels with beauty rings and center caps, the impact of the wheels and tires on the overall look of your rod can't be overstated.

You want to get the wheels and tires clean. More than clean, you want them to look as good as they did when they were new. In the case of tires, the maintenance you give them during the detailing process will help determine how long they last and how good they look.

Wheels

There is a vast array of wheel materials and styles used on street rods today.

The wheels on your rod might be made of steel or aluminum. Aluminum wheels can be cast or billet; the finish might be brushed, polished, anodized, or clear-coated. Steel wheels come in chrome or paint, solid or spoked, and a thousand other styles. Along with all the different types of wheels on the market, there are a variety of products to clean them. Each seems to be "guaranteed best." Finding the right product is just not as simple as it used to be. Finding the correct product to clean your wheels means first understanding what you have on the car and then matching your wheel to the best available product.

The Many Types of Wheels and Wheel Cleaners Available

There was a time when wheels were either steel factory-type wheels or mag wheels. No one seemed to worry too much about special cleaners for special wheels. Today, there are at least four distinct types of wheels commonly used on street rods. The cleaners and polish used on one type of wheel won't work very well on another and may even damage the wheel.

When possible, take the wheels off the car for detailing. The first step for these aluminum Weld wheels is a good cleaning with soap and water.

49

After the wheel is clean, it's time to start the detailing and polishing. Eric uses Mothers Mag and Aluminum Polish on these satin-finish wheels. Be sure to match the polish you use to the material and surface being polished.

The large rear wheels and tires are detailed on the car. More of the Mothers polish and a clean terry cloth towel are used to bring out a nice finish.

Much like reading the label prior to buying a polish for your paint, you have to read the wheel cleaner label to ensure the right match between wheel and cleaner. When in doubt about which cleaner to use, stick with the "milder is better" approach. Start with an all-purpose cleaner, and use the stronger cleaners intended for a particular type of wheel only if necessary.

Remember that many of these wheel cleaning products are acid-based. Be sure to wear goggles and gloves if the label recommends them. If the product is a two-part cleaner with a second, neu-

tralizing agent, be sure to follow through with the second step. Don't forget to rinse the driveway thoroughly after using these products so you don't damage any sealer you've put on the asphalt or concrete. Buy a biodegradable product when possible to ensure minimal damage to your grass and the rest of the environment. The sponge or mitt you use for cleaning the wheels should be dedicated to this one rather dirty job.

Finally, some wheels have been sprayed with a clear coat to keep them looking fresh as long as possible. If that is the case, use only mild cleaners

The work was well worth it, as evidenced by the fine shine on this Weld wheel.

These are the products that Dick Cox uses on the wheels and tires of his nice '34 Ford: a tire scrubbing brush, dressing for the tires, and an all-purpose cleaner to cut road grime and rotor dust.

that won't strip off the clear coat. Even the mildest wheel cleaners are designed to remove the dark grey disc brake dust that accumulates on the front wheels of rods with disc brakes.

If you really want to get the wheels clean, they should be removed for the cleaning and detailing operations. And like your car, they should never be cleaned when they're hot because the heat may accelerate the chemical action of the cleaner and harm the finish.

Cleaning Those Wheels

Aluminum wheels—brushed finish

There isn't a lot you can do with brushed finish wheels except get them clean and keep them clean. Assuming there is no clear coat, start with a general-purpose wheel cleaner. If necessary, follow that process with a special mag-style cleaner. Some of these cleaners are acid-based, two-step formulas, with the second step being the neutralizer. A variety of polishes can be used as the final step.

On a brushed-finish wheel, the rough finish means there is little danger in using a product that is too abrasive. When in doubt, try a little of the polish on one small part of a wheel to check the results. At least one professional detailer likes to use a Scotch-Brite pad on brushed aluminum, with a little WD-40 as the final step.

Polished aluminum wheels

Again, beware the clear coat. If the wheels aren't too dirty and oxidized, the general-purpose wheel cleaner will most likely clean off the dirt and brake dust. If the wheels are very dirty and oxidized, an application of liquid cleaner intended for polished wheels (available from a number of manufacturers) may be needed. A toothbrush will aid in scrubbing those hard-to-reach areas near the center cap or around the valve stem. Because this is a polished surface, you probably want to enhance the shine with some polish on a cotton cloth.

Be careful if the surface is anodized. This process adds color to the aluminum, although the color doesn't go very deep. A cleaning agent that is too strong may bleach and lighten the color. Polish-

The first step is a general washing with the general-purpose cleaner from Armor All.

After the cleaning, a dressing is applied to the tires. The use of a sponge or special applicator will keep the dressing off the wheel and fender.

ing an anodized surface is dangerous, as the polish might wear through the thin anodized layer.

When considering the type of polish to use on your wheels, remember that the finer the finish, the more critical the choice of polish becomes. A rough-cast wheel probably won't be harmed if the abrasive used on it is a little too coarse. A polished or chrome-plated wheel, however, will readily show the scratches if a coarse polishing material is used on the smooth surface. When in doubt, use a very fine polish and test it on one small part of the wheel (or the back side) before going on to the other wheels.

Chrome-plated steel wheels

Chrome-plated steel wheels can be treated much like the polished aluminum wheels. Use a general-purpose wheel cleaner to start, followed by a stronger product only if there's a little rust or oxidation you can't remove. After the wheel is really clean, you can polish the wheel with a high-quality, very fine polishing compound designed for chrome-plated surfaces. A cleaner/wax works well here and leaves that protective wax film.

Wire wheels

Wire wheels look great, especially when they are sparkling clean. The trouble is, they can be a lot of work to keep clean. If the dirt and dust layer is only light, then the one-size-fits-all wheel cleaner will probably do the job. In order to get into all the areas between the spokes, you will need the toothbrush and the small paintbrush. Some detailers use the bench grinder to make an even narrower toothbrush—one that gets between the spokes. Polishing all those chrome spokes is a lot of work. A better compromise might be cleaner/wax, though even that means using most of your available elbow grease.

Factory steel wheels with beauty rims and center caps

More and more street rodders are running a factory Chevrolet or Mopar slotted steel wheel with beauty rings and a small cap (either the factory cap or a simple baby-moon) in the center. Detailing these is a matter of first removing the ring and center cap and then washing the wheel underneath. Unless the

Dick likes Semichrome polish for his brushed-finish aluminum wheels. Here the polish is applied to a clean cotton diaper.

These wheels never get very dirty, and it only took a little work to restore the shine and finish. Dick notes that too much work with the polish will eliminate the brushed finish and leave the wheels with a smooth finish instead.

brake dust is heavy, a simple soap-and-water solution may be all that's needed. After cleaning the rim, get a can of spray paint in the correct color and touch up any areas with chipped or missing paint. When the paint is dry, use a little polish on each wheel followed by a coat of wax to give the wheel some protection and a nice shine.

Each beauty ring and center cap should be washed and polished or given the once-over with some cleaner/wax. All this attention given to the individual wheel parts gets to be a lot of work—but it's all worth it when the wheels are back on the car and sparkling bright as you drive down the street.

Tires

You would think that something as simple as a tire would be simple to clean. Nothing could be further from the truth. There are numerous tire cleaners and dressings on the shelves of your local parts store and more than a little controversy about which is the best product or type of product.

Do you want tires that look new? Or tires that look better than new? Do you want them black, or inky black, shiny black, or matte black? And you thought this part would be easy.

Available Products and Methods of Application

What you want are tires that look fresh and new, with just enough shine. The start, of course, is a good cleaning. The first layer of dirt and brake dust probably came off when you cleaned the wheels. The next step should be a cleaner meant for tires—

A little demonstration project that started with the worst of all possible wheels, two from a certain well-worn Henry J.

Nothing more high-tech than soap and water. In this case, Spic and Span was used for the initial cleaning of the wheel and tire.

After the initial wash it's time to start with the Scotch-Brite pad. The pad is used wet to help remove stains as well as oxidation.

The wheel is starting to pick up a nice soft shine after all that scrubbing and polishing with the Scotch-Brite pad.

The applicator helps to keep the tire dressing on the tire and not on the wheel.

Don't give up on those old swap meet rims, the ones that have been in the basement for five years. The tire needs another application of dressing, but otherwise, the difference in the two rims is pretty encouraging.

one of the variety found on the store shelf. Whitewall cleaners work on blackwall tires, too. Just follow the directions. Most tire cleaners need to be sprayed on and left in place for a few minutes. If the tires are dirty, you will want to scrub them well with a short-bristle brush before rinsing off the cleaner.

Some people wash the tires after the wheels, using a cardboard masking template to keep the tire-cleaning products off the wheel. You can use a sponge or special applicator to get the cleaner on the tire without getting too much on the wheel.

After a good cleaning, you can apply the tire dressing of your choice. There are about a million dressings on the market. Each one has a good brand name and is promoted as the best. There is more than a little controversy about which of these products is really the best. Steve Lindsey at S&R Detailing would say only that he prefers a "petroleum-based dressing [as opposed to water-based products] because they seem to last longer."

The one thing everyone seems to agree on is the need for an applicator. Similar to a small sponge connected to a tube, applicators are a good way to get the dressing on the tire and only on the tire (as opposed to spray applicators that put the dressing on the tire, the wheel, and the fender lip). A folded towel or a clean sponge could be used here too.

Everyone has their own idea on how shiny the tires should be. Most of the dressings need to be

A little Deuce coupe with chrome reverse wheels. All you need is soap and water or maybe some basic wheel cleaner followed by cleaner/wax or chrome polish.

An unusual aluminum wheel (actually this is the backside of a wheel turned around) with lots of the proverbial nooks   *and crannies just crying for a small, stiff, bristle brush and some aluminum wheel cleaner.*

Steel wheels with center caps need the simple soap-and-water treatment, a little touch-up paint perhaps, and a separate polishing operation for the center cap.

You have to know what you want when you go out in search for a wheel care product because the shelves are loaded with products to fit every conceivable need.

Eagle One markets a successful line of wheel care products with separate products for different types of wheels. An all-purpose wheel cleaner is usually the mildest and often a good place to start with your wheel detailing.

The low-tech answer to brushed aluminum wheels in need of cleaning and polishing, Scotch-Brite pads are available in two levels of coarseness. The WD-40 leaves a nice shine on the wheels.

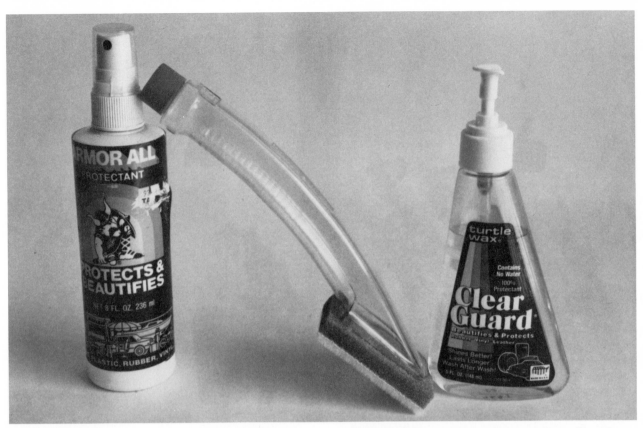

A variety of dressings are available from the auto parts store. Applying them to the tire and not the wheel and fender is made much easier with an applicator like this one from One Grand.

Boyd Coddington—Mr. Street Rod Wheel—brings us a new line of wheel care and car care products. The Wheel Cleaner is a mild product that can be used on any type of wheel. The tire dressing is designed as a penetrant rather than a sealer and gives the tires a "new" look.

More wheel care products. This one is part of the expanded line from Mothers. Be sure to read the labels; this product is a one-step cleaner for nearly any type of wheel.

Mothers is the mag wheel and and aluminum polish. It works fine on most aluminum surfaces but not on chrome plate. A polish must be matched to the metal and the metal's finish.

buffed a little following the application. You have some control over the shine, depending on how much you "polish" the tire. Each product produces a slightly different finish, and that finish may differ from one brand of tire to another (because each rubber compound is unique).

Finding the right tire dressing is, in part, a matter of trial and error. Try a few that come recommended by friends and choose the one that gives the correct "blackness" for your personal taste.

Finally

Getting those Boyd's wheels and T/A tires really clean turns out to be just as much work as detailing the body. But the results are worth it. When you're all done, the wheels will roll with a certain sparkle, polished to a perfect finish. That finish will contrast nicely with your tires, the really black tires with no stains and no weather-checking on the sidewall.

Chapter 5

Interior Detailing

Introduction

The products and methods used in cleaning and detailing the interior on your hot rod or street rod will vary depending on the materials used. Seats may be covered with cloth, vinyl, leather, or a combination of two materials. Dashboards come in everything from plastic to steel to brushed aluminum. Because there are so many different materials used in the interior of a modern street rod, your first interior detailing will require more than just soap and water. A little experimentation is required to find a good match between your interior, the materials of which it's made, and the products available to clean the carpet, seats, glass, and all the rest.

Making Sense of All Those Products

Making sense of all the products on the shelf of the local parts store can be very confusing. For starters, you need the basics: A good vacuum cleaner, a sponge or two dedicated to interior work, at least one small brush for scrubbing carpet and seats, and of course, some clean towels. The cleaners you choose will depend on the materials at hand.

A good interior detailing starts with the vacuum cleaner. Here, Eric starts on the inside of Dick's '34 Ford. This is the same garage where Dick washes the car—without a floor drain.

A conventional home-style vacuum cleaner will work fine if the carpet isn't badly soiled and if you don't intend to get the carpet or seats very wet during the shampooing process.

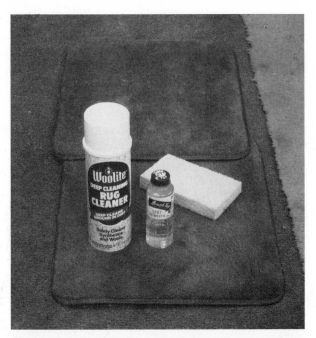

A good carpet shampoo and a stain remover are all you need to clean most carpets.

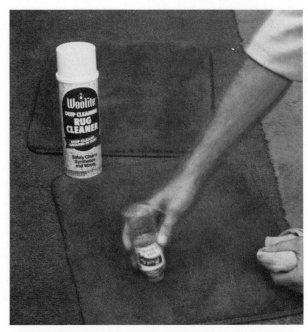

A small grease stain is removed with the spot remover.

You probably need ammonia, spray carpet cleaner, soap and water, spot remover, and some cleaner/wax.

The Carpet

There aren't many rods with rubber floor mats these days. Cleaning the carpet on your rod starts with a good thorough vacuuming. If you don't have a good shop vacuum at home, you might want to use the super-suck at the local self-service car wash.

Pull out the floor mats and start in with the vacuum. Pull the seats forward and vacuum the area behind the seats. Be sure to get under the front seats before moving them back. Spend a little extra time here and go over the carpet more than once, moving the vacuum nozzle in different directions each time. Try to pull as much dirt as you can from the carpet before starting with the shampoo.

A smaller nozzle made from plastic will aid in getting under the seats, behind the pedals, and all those other hard-to-reach areas. If you're working in your home shop, an air nozzle tied to the air compressor will help in dislodging dirt and crud that gets stuck in the seat rails or down between the seats—areas you can't reach even with the small plastic nozzle on the vacuum cleaner.

The seats will have to be vacuumed, too, before they can be cleaned, so you might want to jump in now and vacuum the seats. If they're covered in cloth, spend some time as you did with the carpet and try to dislodge as much dirt as possible. Get down into the crack between the seat cushion and the back and clean out as much of the old popcorn and as many of the gum wrappers as you can. If your

After taking out the stains the mats looked so good that Eric decided to simply sponge them down with an ammonia-and-water solution.

Like any shampoo, the solution must be worked into the carpet for good cleaning. A small brush works well with the aerosol shampoos.

The problem with most wet-and-dry vacuums is the floor space they take up in a small shop. This is a nice, small model that can eliminate any worry about vacuuming moisture off the carpet and mats.

car is a two-door, be sure to flip forward each front bucket seat and clean out the hinge area.

A soft brush attachment on the vacuum can sometimes be used to pull dirt and dust from the A/C and fresh air vents. Don't forget the area around the console and floor shift; these are usually great dirt collectors.

The floor mats will need to be vacuumed too. These are actually easier than the carpet since they can be taken out of the car and slapped on the ground a time or two in order to loosen the dirt and grime. Be sure to clean the nozzle of the vacuum occasionally, especially when going from the carpet to the seat, so dirt from the floor isn't transferred to the seats.

Shampoo

The shampoo you use mostly depends on how dirty the carpet is. The shelves at the grocery store are stocked with a wealth of brand-name products intended to shampoo a small area of carpeting. Most of these don't really soak the carpet but rather just wet the top nap of the carpet. For problem areas, there are spot removers, and for really dirty carpet there are heavy-duty cleaners.

For the street rodder who keeps his or her interior very clean, a simple treatment with ammonia and water may be all that is required. The ammonia should be mixed four capfuls to a half gallon of warm water. With a clean sponge, wet the carpet with the ammonia-water mixture. Do not let it drip as you work your way over the carpet, wiping as you go. Traffic areas may need more than one treatment. After the carpet has dried, vacuum it one more time. Floor mats should get the same treatment, with spot remover for those small stains.

During those times when you don't want to do a full shampoo of the carpet, baking soda can be used as a dry shampoo. Just spread it liberally over the carpet and work it in with a small brush. Allow it to sit at least thirty minutes and then do a good vacuuming job. The baking soda will help to pull dirt from the carpet and has the added advantage of eliminating odors without the use of those obnoxious little skunks and pine trees that hang below the dash.

Dirtier carpet may require a product like Turtle Wax Carpet Cleaner or Woolite Rug Cleaner. Most of these products instruct you to spray the shampoo on the carpet and then work it into the nap with a damp sponge. (A brush can also be used to do a better job of working the shampoo into the carpet.) After it

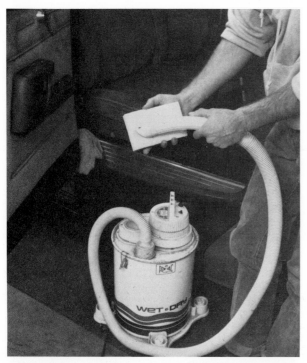

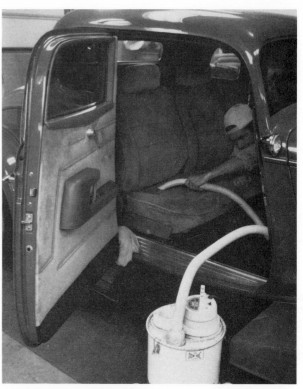

The vacuum nozzle picks up a lot of dirt during the carpet cleaning phase. It's important to wipe off the nozzle before moving on to the seats so that dirt isn't transferred to the seats.

Cleaning the seats starts with a thorough vacuuming, including all the cracks and crevices.

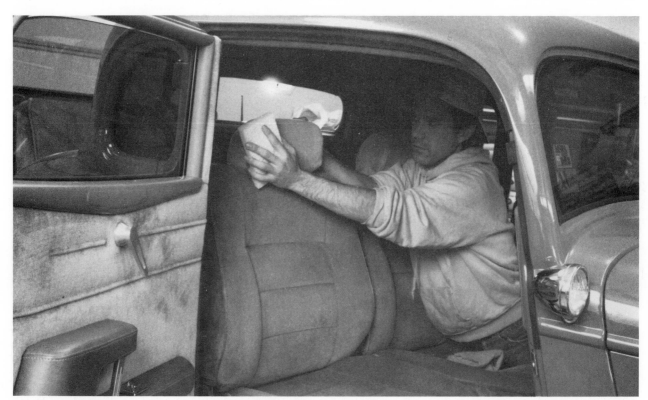

The fabric-covered seats in Dick's '34 weren't very dirty and were cleaned with a clean sponge using ammonia and water.

dries, vacuum up all the dirt with a good wet-and-dry vacuum.

The dirtier the carpet is, the more you need to scrub it and the wetter the carpet becomes. Mildew becomes a potential problem, so when you're all through, be sure to put the car in the sun with the doors open so everything can dry completely.

Some people dislike the commercial, off-the-shelf cleaners because they leave behind a sticky residue. A once-over with a clean sponge dipped in the ammonia solution—used after you use the commercial shampoo—will remove any residue and leave the carpets and mats really clean.

While you're down there on the floor, look over the metal strips at the edge of the carpet. At the very least, these should be wiped down with ammonia and a sponge. If they're really beat up, a little polish or brushing with a Scotch-Brite pad will restore their original brightness and finish. Take a minute and clean the heads on the Phillips screws with a toothbrush at the same time.

The console also needs a little attention at this time. If there's a boot around the shifter, it probably needs to be wiped down with a leather/vinyl cleaner and treated with a dressing. The console itself probably requires a simple cleaning.

Before getting up off your knees, take a brush and clean the pedals. Rubber surfaces can be

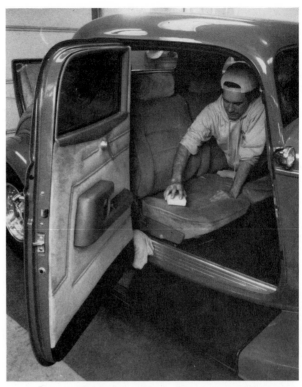

The ammonia-and-water solution works well on fabric that isn't badly soiled and leaves no residue behind.

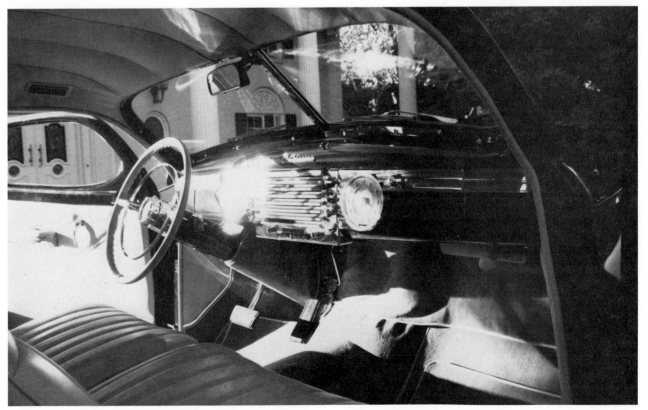

Not a typical street rod interior, this Doug Thompson-built '47 Packard is all leather and chrome. It calls for cleaner/ wax on the dash and Lexol (or another good leather cleaner) and conditioner for the seats and door panels.

Far-Out Gary applies a Spray-and-Vac type shampoo product on the seat of a '47 Chevy pickup truck.

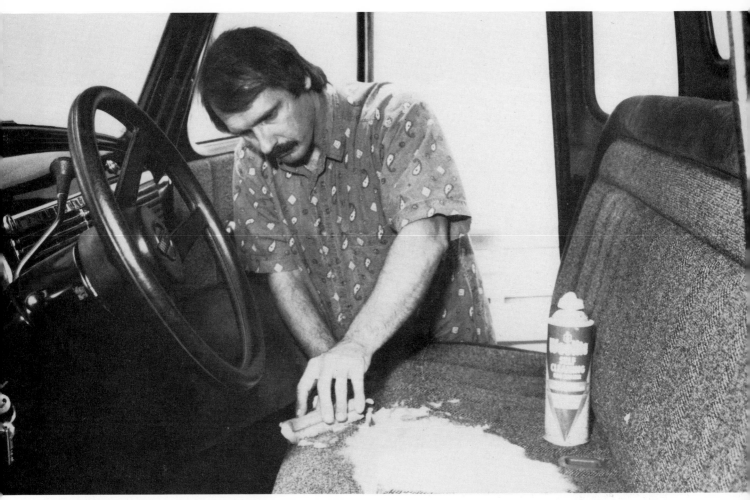

The Woolite is worked into the seat fabric with a small brush. After treating the entire seat, the shampoo will be *allowed to dry and then vacuumed off, pulling the dirt off with it.*

cleaned with a little ammonia or general-purpose cleaner and a brush to get the dirt out of the ribs. Metal trim can be shined up with the appropriate polish, and finally, the pedals get a squirt of dressing to keep them looking nice.

The Seats

The soap, cleaner, or shampoo you use to clean your seats will depend on the type of material covering them. Cloth seats, perhaps the most common type, can be cleaned much as you did the carpet. First, they need a good vacuuming. If they are pretty clean, a wipe-down with the ammonia and water solution may be all that is needed. Use a damp sponge, preferably not the same one you used to clean the dirty carpet.

Dirtier seats will need shampoo. The same products used on the carpet will work on the cloth-covered seats. Again, use a damp sponge or brush to work the foam into the seat covering. Try not to get the seat any wetter than necessary so the seat will eventually dry. A good wet-and-dry vacuum will

help, too, not only for dirt removal but for pulling as much moisture from the seat as possible.

You may want to wipe down the clean seat with the ammonia solution to eliminate any residue left by the shampoo. Don't forget to clean (polish if appropriate) the plastic or metal trim at the lower edges of the seat.

Leather Seats

In a class all by themselves, good leather seats will last the life of the car if taken care of properly. Leather is a most durable material, yet the environment of an automobile, with its temperature extremes, means that without maintenance, even the best of hides will crack and fade over time.

The first object, of course, is to clean the leather. If the soiling is very mild, the seats can be cleaned with that old favorite, ammonia and water. More thorough cleaning should be done with a well-known product meant for leather and leather alone. Lexol is a name that comes up again and again. For cleaning the fine leather seats in your rod, use Lexol

These are some of the items that Steve Anderson keeps in his cleaning kit. The Fiebing's Tan-Kote is found in stores that carry leather goods and tack for horses.

Many modern street rods use seats and door panels covered with two materials. Here Eric applies Tan-Kote to the lower (leather) door panel on Steve's Deuce.

or a similar product. In cases where the seats have become very soiled, something stronger will have to be used, and the logical choice is saddle soap.

Almost as important as the cleaning is the conditioning of the leather that follows. What keeps leather looking good is regular application of a good conditioner. In fact, the oils worked into the leather during the tanning process are what give good leather its supple nature. After a thousand hot and cold cycles in the interior of your car, many of those oils are lost. A good conditioner will replace the oils and leave your seats feeling soft and supple. Although there are plenty of good conditioning products, Lexol comes highly recommended.

Vinyl seats may be the easiest of all to clean and maintain. Because the vinyl is waterproof, there are no worries about getting these seats too wet. Scrub them down with a product made to clean vinyl (Turtle Wax and Meguiar's both make such products) or a general-purpose cleaner. Use a brush to work the soap over the surface of the seats, and then wipe them down with clean terry cloths. Work one section of the seat at a time, and move on after that section is clean and wiped down. You can go over the seams and stitching with a toothbrush if the material has gotten pretty dirty. Vinyl would seem to be so tough that it shouldn't make any difference what you used to wash it, but in reality, soap or solvent that is too strong will pull the color from the

When a hide goes through the tanning process, a lot of oils are worked into the leather. In the hot interior of a car, many of those oils are lost. The regular use of a leather conditioner will help to replace those oils and keep the leather soft and pliable.

Eric wipes down the leather-covered armrest with simple ammonia and water because it isn't very dirty. Dirtier leather needs a product like Lexol, or in very dirty cases, some saddle soap. Leather cleaning should always be followed by the application of a good leather conditioner.

vinyl. Stick with soap and water (not too strong) or a product meant for cleaning vinyl.

Much like their more expensive counterparts, vinyl seats benefit from a good conditioner almost as much as leather seats do. The choices for dressings are too numerous to mention. Professional detailers prefer a petroleum-based product since these seem to last longer. Most products meant to condition and restore leather will also work to restore and put the oils back in vinyl. However, don't do the reverse and use vinyl products on leather.

The Headliner

Headliners seldom get very dirty—and it's a good thing because they're harder than the devil to clean. Cleaning with too much vigor can result in their destruction rather than their cleaning.

Less is more in this case. Bad stains can probably be removed with a dry cleaning formula available at most auto parts stores or at the grocery store. For most situations a simple wipe-down will suffice. Wet your sponge with a little ammonia and water or a general-purpose cleaner, wipe the headliner and be done with it. Avoid the temptation to get it *really* clean.

The Dashboard

A metal dash needs to be cleaned with a good general-purpose cleaner that is applied with a clean sponge and wiped off with a terry towel. Leather- and vinyl-covered dashboards will need to be cleaned with products mentioned earlier for cleaning leathers and vinyl seats. It is helpful to apply the materials to the dash using an applicator or sponge, since spraying them directly on the dash will also spray them all over the inside of the windshield.

The face of the dash presents more challenges. The chromed wonder in a 1948 Buick will require a general cleaning followed by some TLC. Careful cleaning with a towel and some Q-tips will clean all

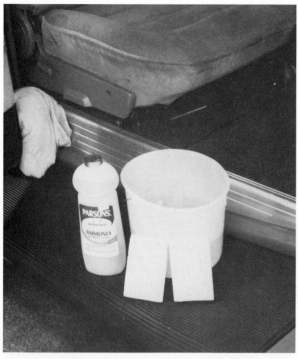

That old favorite, ammonia and water, works well to clean the rubber-covered running board as well as the sill plate.

A sponge works well in cleaning the running boards. Don't skimp on sponges; buy a pack and use fresh ones often to avoid any chance of leaving dirt behind.

Be sure to wipe down the sill plate and door jamb area. You might want to apply some wax to the painted areas and a little polish to the metal plate.

the small seams and the areas between the grille bars. Follow up the cleaning with a coat of cleaner/wax, and the shine will be downright dazzling. Meguiar's makes a special cleaner/wax intended for your interior and dashboard. The dials need to be cleaned with glass cleaner—if they're glass. Plastic polish is available for more modern materials. Sometimes a little plastic polish can make that old scratched up speedometer "glass" look almost like new.

The billet dash in a modern Deuce might need an initial cleaning and then a little brushed-aluminum cleaner or aluminum polish.

Door Panels

Cleaning the door panels is similar to cleaning the seats: if they're fabric, you need shampoo, and if they're leather, you need leather-cleaning products. Some door panels may combine two or three materials, each one requiring different methods and cleaners.

The vacuum cleaner is probably a good place to start. Vacuum the panels, working out as much of the dirt as possible. Cloth panels will probably need

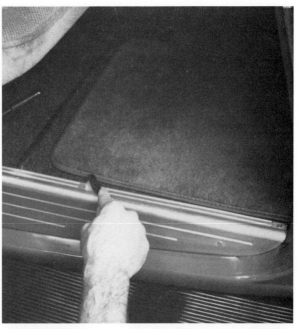

A toothbrush will do a nice job of cleaning all the crud that accumulates in these Phillips head screws.

The cleaning products used on the dash depend on what it's made of. This Wabbit's wood dash is wiped down with Murphy's Oil Soap, a common household cleaner.

Take it One Step at a Time

Among all the world's professional detailers there are very few who detail street rods, and even fewer who specialize in rods and classic cars. Gary "Far-Out" Humenik is one such man. For almost twenty years Gary has been spending his evenings and Saturday afternoons detailing cars for some of the little shows on the West Coast. "Little" shows like Pebble Beach and Oakland. Though he never advertises and doesn't even have a business card, Gary stays very busy. In fact, Gary detailed nine of the last ten Oakland Roadster Show winners. Far-Out Gary is the one man who understands the special detailing needs of street rodders.

Where do you start when you detail a street rod?

I like to start by taking the hood off the car and then doing the motor first. Motors are first because they get the dirtiest. If the motor is pretty dirty, I spray it down with Gunk. After rinsing it off I like to spray the engine down with Marvel Mystery Oil. I usually let it soak in overnight and then rinse it off the next day. It doesn't hurt the wires or the distributor cap. The Mystery Oil works especially well if the engine has a lot of aluminum accessories; that Mystery Oil really gets down into the pores of the aluminum and makes all that stuff look brand new. Simple Green works the same way.

What do you use to really polish and detail the engine after it's clean?

I like a good metal polish—I like Blue Magic—for the chrome stuff. Brasso on a radiator. Anodized aluminum cleans up with Pledge. Billet that isn't anodized needs a Scotch-Brite pad and some WD-40. WD-40 works well on turbochargers too. Some people don't like the WD-40 because it leaves a film, and the film attracts dirt. On stainless headers I use a Scotch-Brite pad, if they have a brushed finish. If the headers are polished, I use some stuff called Blue-away, which they sell at the motorcycle stores. A good idea is to paint the inside of the headers with some heat paint before they are bolted on the car. It insulates the pipes and prevents a lot of the blue color.

What kind of soap do you recommend for use on the car body?

I wash the car with any car-wash shampoo. Boyd has some new products out, and there are plenty of others. In terms of what kind of sponge or whatever, I like to use wash mitts or an old piece of a towel. A chamois always seems to leave streaks. I like an old terry-cloth towel that's been treated with fabric softener.

What do you like to use for a polish or glaze after washing the car?

I start with a rubbing compound. I mask off all the edges so I won't rub through. Then I use a fine cutting pad and a 1700rpm buffer. Then I go over it by hand to eliminate any buffing marks, and I take some Meguiar's number seven and go over it again by hand.

Can someone who is not experienced use a rubbing compound and a buffer?

Probably not. They can probably do a good job with a mild polish like Meguiar's number seven. They can follow that with a glaze like the number nine. Some people think they are finished after they use a product like the seven or nine. But those are not waxes.

How do you feel about waxes, and which is the best type?

People should always use a carnauba paste wax. It helps the shine, it makes the car wash easier. I wax the whole car, I even wax the windows because they look better, and any water that hits them just rolls right off. I use a new wax applicator pad for each car. I also don't let the wax dry. I do a small area and take the wax off right away. That way the wax isn't dry

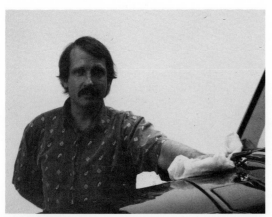

Gary Far-Out Humenik detailed nine of the last ten Oakland Roadster Show winners. In almost twenty years of detailing street rods and classic cars, he has discovered quite a few unique detailing tricks.

Gary's new shop is very well lit and super sanitary. Note the small, portable fluorescent light for working along the sides of the car.

These are the tools and products (at least some of them) that Gary keeps at hand. Note the open-weave cotton material for waxing and hand polishing, the Scotch-Brite pad, the pipe cleaners, and the masking tape he uses to mask off seams and openings during application of the wax.

and hard to take off. It means I'm not pushing real hard on the paint and creating new scratches. I wax up to the edge, but at the edge or seam I just run the rag or applicator over it lightly and let the residue on the rag put a little wax on the seam or edge. That way you don't get as much dry, white residue in the edges. It's easier to eliminate the problem than to go over the car with a toothbrush or toothpick later. A toothpick can put more scratches in the paint. You can also use ¹/₈in masking tape on edges to eliminate the problem altogether.

Do you take any special precautions with clear-coat paints?

I don't worry about it, especially if it's a urethane clear coat. It's so darned hard that I just take the normal precautions when I'm rubbing on an edge, otherwise, I don't worry about it. If it's a urethane job, I work with the painter and we try to do any finish sanding before the paint ages completely because the paint gets so hard. I'm more careful with lacquer because it's a lot softer.

Should an amateur try to do the color sanding and the buffing after a fresh paint job?

I recommend that they don't. I think the sanding and buffing done after the paint job determine how that paint job will ultimately look. If you aren't careful you can put scratches in the paint. Even if the paint job doesn't get ruined, an amateur probably won't get all the shine available from a certain paint job. If you get a good paint job and have it buffed out correctly, you will have a great paint job with good shine. All the

owner will have to do is detail that paint job two or three times a year, and it will look great for a long time.

What about convertible tops?

I like to mix up some Tide for a canvas top. I put it on with a short bristle brush. I take the top off when I can. Otherwise, I use sheets of plastic taped over the window area to keep the water out of a roadster. For the rear window—if it's plastic—my advice is to never, never, never touch that rear window. If it gets scratched you can use a polish on it, but it's easier to just stay away from it in the first place.

There are a variety of materials and styles of wheels commonly used on rods today. How do you handle the various aluminum and steel wheels, and what do you use on tires?

Wheels and tires are a real art. Each wheel is different, and each rubber compound is different.

I start by washing the wheels and tires with some kind of cleaner that will cut the grime and brake dust. Then, if the wheels are brushed, I use a Scotch-Brite red or green pad, depending on what kind of finish the wheel has. For a show, a light coat of WD-40 really gives them a nice soft shine. On a polished or chrome rim I use a good metal polish.

For the tires, I use Black Chrome or No Touch. There are plenty of other products that work just fine, too. It depends on what kind of finish you want. For a photo session, shiny tires look better, but for day to

continued on next page

day or for show, a matte black finish looks more natural.

On wire wheels I use glass wax. I use a toothbrush that I grind down to get into the little crevices. After the wax has been on for a little while, I wipe it off. The glass wax has some cleaner in it, and it leaves a high sheen and protects the wheel.

How do you feel about interiors? What about the different materials?

On leather I like to use Lexol. It seems to work. It dries naturally. On cloth upholstery I use a Spray and Vac-type product—any of the good brand names you see at the store. It's important to vacuum really well afterward.

There isn't anything you can do for felt headliners. Light vacuuming, maybe, but that's about all.

For carpet, you can use a spot remover for the real dirty areas. Spray and vac will work, too.

Black Chrome works well on dashboards. Lots of Q-tips on A/C outlets. Remember, what you think people won't see, they always do. Doorjambs, too. Be sure they're really clean, especially the bottom—that's what people see. I usually polish the bottom edge of the doorjamb.

How about cleaning a chassis?

With a really fancy chassis, I like to Gunk the suspension too, especially if it's a full independent chassis. Then I get underneath and wipe everything down. When it's clean, I go over it with wax so it looks good and the dirt doesn't stick. With anodized stuff, again, Pledge works real well. If there's a leak, of course, then everything is a lot harder to clean. Especially an antifreeze leak. Antifreeze on polished aluminum, like a water pump, will make a stain you can't remove. Some people will put a clear coat on a polished part before they bolt it on the engine and that eliminates the problem.

I usually don't wax frames unless the finish is really smooth. If the metal is kind of rough, you can't wipe all the wax off, and it looks terrible.

What do you use for paint chips?

I use a match stick—assuming it's a solid color car—and put on multiple layers. I allow each one to dry, then smooth it down with real fine grit sandpaper and a little polish.

Are there any other tricks you've learned?

Just one good one for storage. When the car is in storage, everything weathers and oxidizes, and the car needs a lot of cleanup when it comes out in the spring. A light coat of Vaseline on the tires, trim, wheels, and anything else will seal those parts from the air and prevent oxidation. When the car comes out of storage, just wipe off the Vaseline, and the parts look just like they did when you put the car away. It saves a lot of cleanup and polishing work.

What are the mistakes people make when they detail their cars?

I would say they get tired about halfway through, and then they get sloppy at the end. They tend to use the wrong rags. They wax the car in the sun.

What is the secret to good street rod detailing?

The secret to good detailing is taking your time. Spend the time on the areas where you don't think people will look. Take the time to clean the plug wires, line up all the screw heads; don't skip those little things. There really is no easy way. You have to do it all, do it thoroughly, and do it one step at a time.

The metal dash in Ray Bozarth's custom Buick will need cleaner/wax and some good chrome polish to make it really shine.

some of the same shampoo used on the seats. The armrests tend to be the dirtiest single item on the door panel. Maybe the door panels only need to be wiped down with ammonia and water while the armrests need a good shampooing.

If the armrests are leather, they will need to be cleaned with Lexol or another good leather cleaner. Remember to treat all the leather in the car with a good leather conditioner.

The door handles and any chrome or stainless trim on the door panels will need to be wiped off first with a general-purpose cleaner. If the handles have a ribbed design, the toothbrush may be a good way to clean down into those crevices. When the handles are clean, wipe them down with some cleaner/wax and give them a quick buff. If the door handles and window cranks (and the escutcheons behind the handles) are especially dirty, they should be removed and soaked in a general-purpose cleaner or dishwashing detergent. Far-Out Gary's neat trick for aluminum engine parts would work well on billet door handles and window cranks—a good soaking in Marvel Mystery Oil or Simple Green to make them look like new.

Cleaning the glass includes removal of all those tacky, sticky stickers. A razor blade makes a good start.

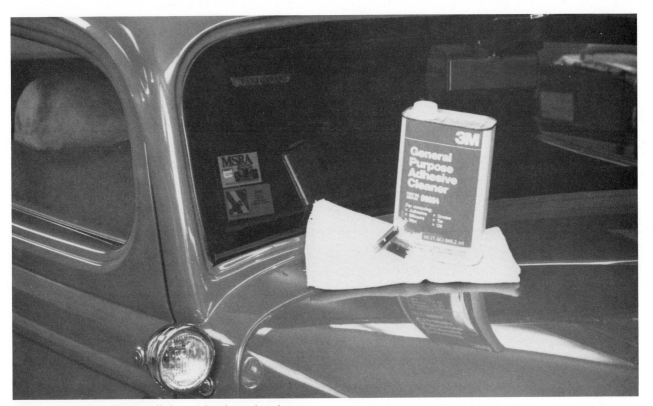

The razor blade will take off the sticker but often leaves behind the adhesive. Cleaning off the adhesive is made much simpler with a little cleaner like this product by 3M.

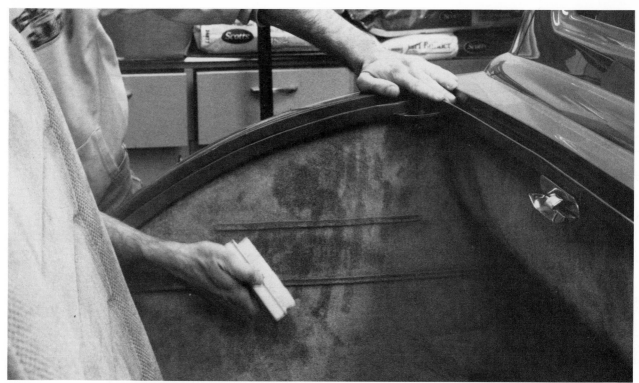

The fabric of your interior can be clean and still look bad if the nap carries what looks like dirty handprints. Use a small brush to brush the nap.

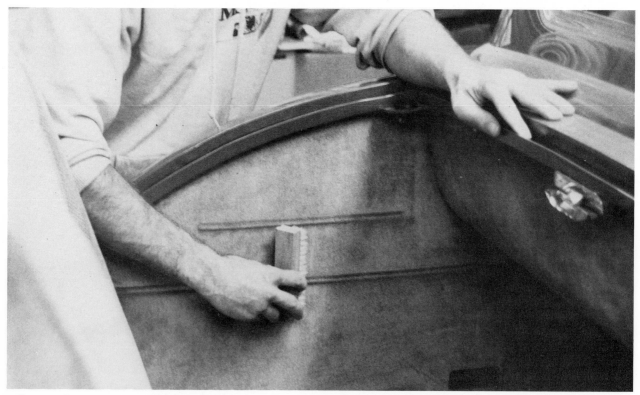

Following the use of a small brush, the nap runs in one direction and the interior looks great.

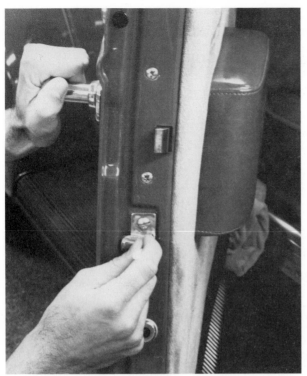

A Q-tip and some cleaner or polish can be used to clean the latches and screws on the door itself.

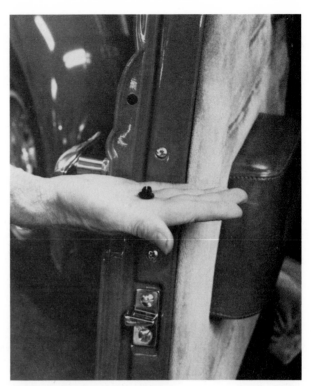

Details, details. These little plugs are a nice touch, giving this '34 Ford door a nice finished look.

Seatbelts

Highly visible though often overlooked, the seatbelts need to be cleaned along with all the other interior components. The belts themselves can be cleaned with shampoo or simple soap and water, using a brush to work the soap into the belt. Most manufacturers recommend that solvents never be used on the belt for fear that the strength and integrity of the belt might be compromised. Pull the belts out of their retractors and keep them out with a string or bungee cord tied to the steering wheel or something else handy. A towel placed under the belt will keep the soap and water from getting all over the seats. After the belts are clean, take a minute and apply a little cleaner/wax to the seatbelt buckles to give them a nice shine.

Windshield and Side Glass

Just when you think the interior is all done, there's still the glass to clean. This is another area where opinions differ sharply in regard to which is the best product and method for cleaning glass. Household glass cleaners such as Windex do a good job, and it seems everyone has a favorite. Some people insist on a product with ammonia, or simply an ammonia and water solution. If no one in the family is a smoker and the glass never gets very dirty,

plain water may work just fine.

A squirt bottle will put the cleaner of your choice on the glass, although it may put the cleaner on the dash as well. A small, clean sponge or a towel that has been sprayed with cleaner (you might try an applicator like that used to apply dressings to tires and dashboards) will do a better job of aiming the cleaner on the glass and nowhere else. After washing the window with the damp towel, wipe it down with another clean terry towel. Any buildup of dirt in the corners of the glass can be removed with the toothbrush or Q-tip.

Stickers, those nasty gummy things that we all end up with on our windows after a trip to Oklahoma or Kalamazoo or Bakersfield or wherever, are a real pain to remove completely. Though some people use tape to stick them to the window, most of us end up with some gummy residue in the lower corner of the windshield. A razor blade will take off the sticker, or most of it at least, but there is often a film of goo left behind. Glass cleaner will remove the goo—when combined with a lot of elbow grease. A better answer is adhesive remover like that made by 3M for automobiles. No more rub, rub, rub. Just peel off as much as you can with a razor blade and then wipe the area with the adhesive remover. Follow up with the glass cleaner for the final cleaning.

Some old-timers like to wash the glass with clean water and then wipe it down with newsprint.

This tasteful dash resides in the '40 Ford built by Gene Younk of Minneapolis, Minnesota. It's almost all leather and calls for lots of TLC and quality leather conditioner.
Rodder's Digest

A woody all the way. Each rod interior presents its own detailing challenge. It all depends on what type of materials were used in building the interior. Rodder's Digest

A fresh interior in an old classic. From the looks of this immaculate interior, someone understands just how to detail this kind of interior. Rodder's Digest

When you detail the interior, don't forget the trunk. If it's as nice as this one, you will want to be sure it looks perfect.
Rodder's Digest

No leather here, just a nice, clean fabric interior and a simple metal dashboard. Rodder's Digest

Among the products offered by One Grand is this dressing designed for interior and exterior vinyl and rubber surfaces. It is said to leave a medium gloss with no yellowing over time.

Meguiar's recently introduced this Medallion leather conditioner for all leather surfaces. Designed to restore oils to the leather, the Medallion is said to provide vital nutrients to the leather and thus help keep it soft and natural.

That's fine except that the new water-based inks often smear. The older inks actually acted as a mild polish and did, indeed, leave the glass looking very good.

If you have water spots or rub marks embedded in the glass, then a little polish is what you need. Eagle One, among others, makes a glass cleaner and polish, and Meguiar's makes a good plastic polish that works on glass as well. In the case of hard-to-remove stains or overspray on the glass, steel wool in a 00 grit can be combined with polish to clean the glass. Beware of the newest acrylic glass offered on new cars. It's a little softer than the glass we've known for years, and can't be cleaned with steel wool.

One of the best-known glass products is Rain-X, which is actually a cleaner and polish. Not only does it leave the glass looking its best, it leaves the glass so smooth that rain drops roll right off. This is especially nice if your hot rod or street rod is still relying on vacuum windshield wipers to push the water off the glass.

Finally

When everything inside the car is as clean as it can be, there is just one more step. One more thing to do before you can walk away with that deep feeling of satisfaction: an application of Scotchgard or a similar product.

83

These are some of the household cleaners we used to detail the interior of Dick Cox's '34 Ford.

Among the expanded line of Mothers car care products is this Upholstery and Carpet Cleaner designed for the automotive market.

Most of these upholstery protectants are petroleum-based products designed to protect the seats and carpet from stains. The protectant is applied as a spray after the seats or carpet is cleaned and dry. You will want to use cardboard panels to mask off other areas of the car where you don't want the protectant sprayed, but otherwise, the application is pretty simple.

Usually one or two applications are all that is required for protection. After application, a few drops of water can be sprayed on the material. If the water beads up, then the cloth is protected. If not, then another application is needed. Determining when the protection has worn off can be checked with the same "water bead" test.

At first, detailing the interior seems like the simplest part of the overall detailing process. After finishing the interior you will probably realize that this is actually more work than the outside of the car—especially if the car is a sedan that sees a lot of use.

Yet, in order to really feel the satisfaction of having a well-detailed car, you have to do a thorough job on the interior. If the outside is clean but the inside is dirty, the effect just isn't the same. A well-detailed interior means more than just good maintenance and good results at shows. It means you get to drive down the street surrounded by your own careful handiwork.

More household products that work in detailing a hot rod or street rod. The spot remover will remove the stubborn stains in the carpet, while the Murphy Oil Soap is useful on wooden surfaces.

Lexol has a two-step process for cleaning and conditioning the leather interior in your street rod. Leather will stay soft only if it is provided with fresh oils by a good conditioner.

Chapter 6

Convertible Tops

Introduction

The convertible top or Carson top on your rod is an essential part of the car, so it needs to be every bit as clean and sparkling as the rest of the body. Though you can't wax a canvas top or polish a vinyl Carson top, you can use some simple methods and common sense to keep them looking as good as possible for as long as possible.

Top materials

There are products meant to clean convertible tops, but the shelves are not bulging with them. Most of the products commonly used on convertible tops come from the grocery store or the shelf under the sink at home where the general-purpose cleaners are kept. The soap you use on your top will depend on what it's made of and how dirty it is.

In the old days all the convertible tops were made from canvas. Today, your top might be covered with one of three different types of canvas, or it might be covered in a vinyl material that closely resembles canvas.

Most of the canvas used today is of a Stayfast or Sonnenland type. These modern materials contain synthetic fibers to provide better UV protection and less shrinkage during the life of the top. The canvas material itself is three layers thick: the canvas is bonded to a rubber membrane and under the rubber membrane is a third layer or liner.

The vinyl-top material is embossed with a fine pattern to resemble canvas. The effect is so complete that most people can't tell the difference until they get up close for a better look.

No matter which material covers your top, a convertible top is a high-maintenance item. If the top gets very dirty, you can't just buff out the paint. You can't even scrub the hell out of it with bleach or solvent for fear of taking the color out of the top or weakening the stitching that holds it together.

The important thing with a convertible top is maintenance. If you don't let it get dirty and stained, you won't have to use harsh chemicals to get it clean. Wash your top on a regular basis. Don't leave it down for long periods. Be sure it's clean before you put it

Washing a convertible top is pretty simple, especially if it hasn't been allowed to get too dirty.

The material on this nice Model A top is one of the new
rubber-backed canvas products, the same material that
Mercedes-Benz uses.

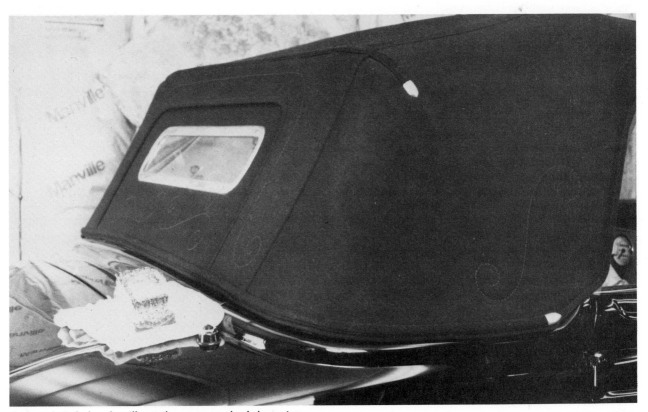

A short-bristle brush will get the soap worked down into
the weave of the fabric.

This window is glass and can be cleaned like any other. Plastic windows are very easy to scratch and should probably just be left alone.

Gene Younk understands the importance of keeping the top clean, especially before it is taken down. Maintenance is the key to a good-looking and long-lasting top. Rodder's Digest

If you're going to advertise your top like this, you had better make sure it's clean. Rodder's Digest

An early, restored roadster like this one belonging to Gene Hetland probably uses the original Hearts-type canvas (without the rubber backing) for the top.

down. Avoid parking under trees, and try to keep the top out of the sun whenever possible.

Staying on Top . . .

If the top on your rod is canvas, the soap you use can come from the laundry room. Most detailers and serious street rodders agree that a mild detergent and a stiff-bristle brush (like the one you use on your fingernails) will do a good job of cleaning a canvas top. Mark Milbrandt, who runs Stitches Upholstery in Minneapolis, likes to use Woolite in warm water to clean a canvas top. The Woolite does a good job of cleaning the canvas yet is mild enough so there is no danger it will attack the fabric or the stitching.

After scrubbing the top, it should be rinsed well so there is no soap residue to create a stain. Bruce Corzine, a roadster owner from Orange County, always takes his top off the car for cleaning. For the washing, Bruce swears by Tide and warm water. After rinsing the top, he insists it be allowed to dry in the sun. Bruce explains that "the sun seems to pull out any wrinkles. It leaves the top looking great, real clean and fresh."

A good drying in the sun will also help eliminate any chance for mold or mildew to develop after the car is put back in the garage. If your canvas top is the old type not backed with rubber, then a treatment with Scotchgard will help to repel water and stains. More likely, yours is made of modern rubber-backed materials, and all you can do is keep it clean.

If the lid on your roadster is covered in vinyl, then there are more choices of which cleanser or soap to use. Though a household detergent may work fine, you can also use a general-purpose cleaner like Formula 409 or Simple Green. You can also use a vinyl cleaner intended primarily for the interior. That same little stiff-bristle brush will help to work the soap down into the pattern of the vinyl and get the top really clean.

The Kent Company makes a two-part convertible top cleaner that includes a granulated cleanser and a sealer that is applied after the top has dried. Westley's lists a convertible top cleaner that is said to remove embedded dirt and stubborn stains. Vinyl tops can be cleaned with some pretty strong materials. But remember that the stronger the cleaner, the greater your risk of pulling the color from the top

A dark top like this one needs extra care during washing since the use of chemicals that are too strong will fade the top prematurely. Rodder's Digest

A variety of common soaps can be used to wash your convertible top.

A vinyl top can withstand stronger soaps than a canvas top, and with less worry about bleaching the material.

Many people use general, all-purpose cleaners on vinyl tops.

A brush with fairly stiff bristles will help to work the soap and water into the weave or pattern of the top.

If you are careful and never let the top get very dirty, you can get it clean with very mild soaps like those seen here—designed for women's wear and intimate apparel.

(not a problem if the top is white) or weakening the stitching.

A badly faded vinyl top can be dyed to restore the color. It's a three-step process that starts with a solvent cleaning, followed by an application of a conditioner, and then the spraying on of the dye. Not quite as nice as a new top, but not as expensive either.

John Moikulak, owner of Motorcar Interiors in Minneapolis, reminds readers that "a convertible top only lasts so long, something like five years—depending on how it's treated and taken care of. The sun fades the tops, and strong chemicals bleach out the color."

So you don't really have a choice. The only thing to do is keep that top clean, because then you won't need to use super-strong chemicals to remove stains. Wash it, and wash it often with a mild soap-and-water solution, and it will not only look good, it will look good for a long period of time.

Chapter 7

Pinstriping

Introduction

If "detailing" can be expanded to include all the little things you do to a street rod to make it really stand out, then pinstriping is definitely part of the process. The idea here is to make the car look good. There's nothing like a few well-placed stripes to really make a car look sharp.

A good paint job needs only a few accents to make it really "jump." A straight yellow paint job might need blue or teal pinstripes to add a little contrast and a lot of accent. Pinstriping lets you get a lot of impact from a small amount of paint.

This pinstriping section covers the essentials of striping. Everything from tape to paint, from design to application. Whether you intend to pay someone else to stripe your rod or be really daring and do it yourself, here is information that will make the task easier.

Most street rodders, even those who insist on doing nearly everything themselves, are reluctant to try pinstriping. Yet, there is no reason that a patient rodder can't do a simple pinstriping job at home.

Design

Choosing the colors and design for the stripes on your car requires experience and taste. If the car

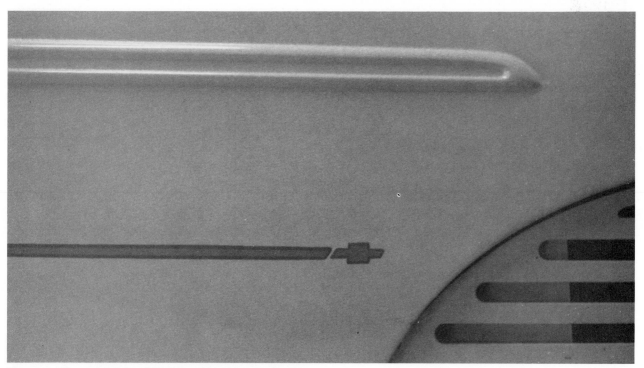

The two-color striping on this Chevrolet adds a lot to the overall design of the car. Little details like this pinstriped Chevrolet symbol add a nice touch.

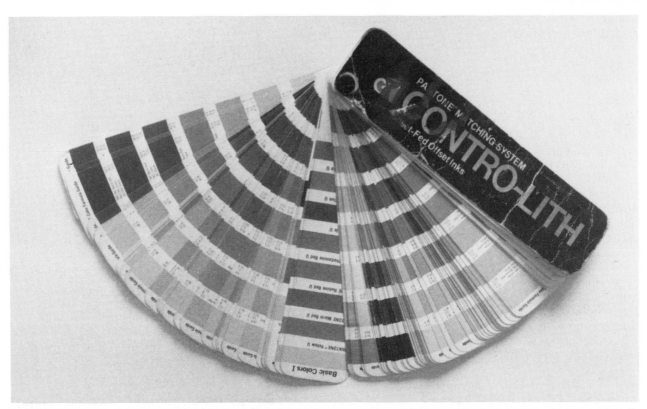

The PMS book is a book of color samples used by commercial printers. It is also a good resource for anyone trying to find a color for pinstripes. It allows you to hold a color or combination of colors up against your car to really see how they work together.

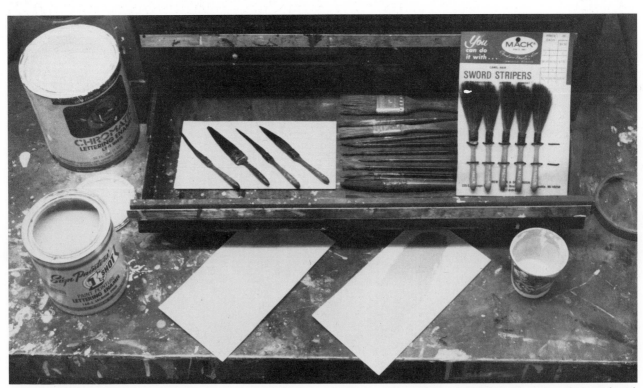

The paintbrushes used for pinstriping look like no other paintbrush. These are from Mack and come in a variety of sizes. They are cleaned after each use and coated with clean oil until their next use.

will be done by a professional pinstriper then the job is easy, just ask him or her for help and advice in the choice of the design and colors. If you're going to do the job yourself, it's a little more difficult.

Short of going back to school to study design, you should probably remember that less is more. This is an accent, not a complete paint job. Besides, you can always go back later and add another line or two. So pick a simple design, just one or two nice stripes that follow the natural lines of the car. Picking the right colors is more difficult. If you have an eye for color, then picking one or two colors to contrast and complement the main color might be an easy task. For the rest of us, there are a few tools to make the job much easier.

Commercial printers use a PMS book as a color guide. Available from a graphic art supply house, the PMS book contains hundreds of color samples and the formulas for making them. Find a color you like and hold it next to the door or quarter panel to see how the two colors look together. Though the book and the formulas are intended for a commercial printer, you will at least get an idea how much of each basic color a particular shade contains. Another

Paint used for pinstriping is designed specifically for that purpose. Here are two of the more common brands, both of which are enamels. Both are designed to go on over any other paint without any reaction. House of Kolor makes striping urethane in typically durable and super-bright colors.

Brian Truesdell of St. Paul, Minnesota, likes to mix the striping paint into small, three-ounce Dixie cups. From the Dixie cup the paint will be applied to a small white card before being brushed onto the car.

Brian has been striping for a number of years and prefers to use a small card to hold the paint. As he pulls the brush through the paint on the card, he has a chance to feel the consistency of the paint. Getting the paint just thick enough is an important part of a good pinstripe job.

good source of color ideas is the paint chip cards available from various paint manufacturers. Although there aren't as many shades as in a PMS book, the color cards are still a good way to try various combinations to see how they work together.

As a final note, many stripers feel that two stripes in two different colors have much more visual impact than a single line or two lines in one color. The two colors, if carefully chosen, work off each other as well as off the color of the car to create more impact.

Tools of the Trade

Pinstriping requires special tools and materials. At the top of the list are the brushes, those funny looking brushes with the short handles and the extra-long bristles. On a good brush those long bristles are usually camel or squirrel hair (most professionals don't like synthetic brushes). The brushes are rated numerically, from 00 to 5, with 00 being the smallest and 5 the biggest. Though the professional might have ten or more brushes in use, the beginner only needs half that many. Three or four brushes from a company such as Mack or Dagger are probably enough to get you started.

Each pinstriper seems to have his or her own formula for cleaning and maintaining his brushes.

The Chevrolet belongs to Jim Kalkes of St. Paul. Brian and Jim have decided to add an additional pinstripe to the Chevy's rear quarter panel. When trying to decide on a design, remember that you can always add a second or third stripe later.

Brian starts by running a quarter-inch piece of masking tape along the surface to act as a guide for the pinstriping.

The masking tape follows the shape of the new pinstripe to come. This tape is used as a guide rather than to mask off an area.

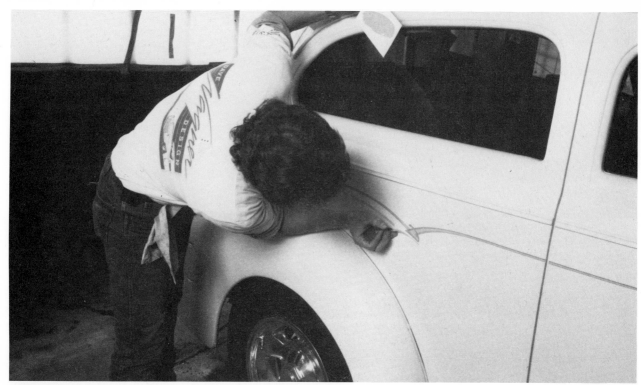

Brian starts near the front of the quarter panel and pulls the brush toward him.

Additional paint is taken from the card; each time Brian is able to feel the consistency of the paint, adding fresh paint or a little thinner as needed.

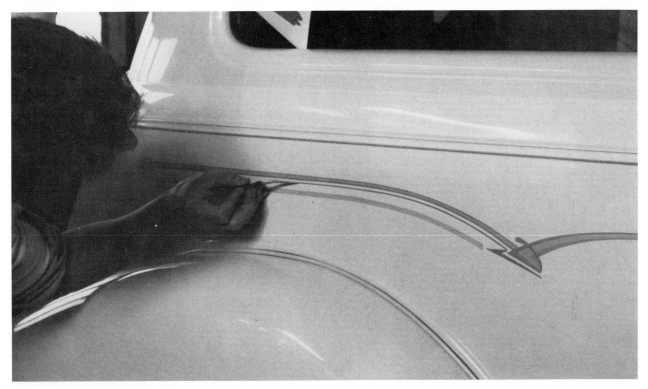

Brian runs his little finger along the guide tape and lays down a perfect stripe.

The stripe is almost finished. Any mistakes can be wiped off with a rag and repainted, especially if the paint is sign painter's enamel.

The finished job. The stripes follow the Chevrolet's natural lines, in part, and the rest is creativity as supplied by Brian Truesdell. Without the stripes, the car would appear very plain.

Brian Truesdell, a well-known striper from St. Paul, Minnesota, likes to clean them with mineral spirits. (He also uses mineral spirits to thin his One-Shot and Chromatic paints.) Brian keeps two cans of mineral spirits on the bench, using the first one to clean most of the paint from the brush and a second can of cleaner spirits for the final cleaning. After cleaning the brushes Brian wets them down with clean engine oil and lays them out flat until they are used again.

Masking tape has a variety of uses in the pinstriping process. Professionals like Brian often use a single piece of quarter-inch masking tape as a guide to follow as they move the brush along the side of the car. Good freehand pinstriping requires years of experience and is probably a no-no for the novice.

The most important thing to remember about masking tape is to always buy a brand name from an auto parts store. All masking tape is not created equal. Some are meant for home use, and some just aren't very good. Use the cheap tape from the discount store and you risk tearing off the original paint when you pull off the tape. Also, 3M manufactures a unique tape product—actually many thin pieces of tape on one roll—that makes the job much simpler. (More on this tape later.)

The paint used for pinstriping is usually a special paint known as sign painter's enamel. This paint is special because it is designed to be inert. Sign painter's enamel can be laid down over the car's paint without any fear that the two paints will react, no matter what type or brand of paint is on the car.

Probably the best-known striping paint is One-Shot Sign Painting Enamel. Another choice is Chromatic Lettering Enamel, which is also designed as an

3M Fine Line Striping tape is like having many thin pieces of masking tape on one roll. The Plastic Tape is useful in *areas where you need to make a lot of bends, as it is more flexible than the conventional masking tapes.*

inert paint. The Chromatic is available in a large range of colors, all designed to be applied over other paints.

Perhaps the brightest and most durable of the striping paints is a product offered by Jon Kosmoski's House of Kolor. Jon's Sign and Lettering Enamel is the only true urethane striping paint, and it offers the durability that only a urethane can achieve. In addition, the House of Kolor paints offer a wide range of bright and wonderful colors. These striping paints can be used as a straight one-coat urethane (with a catalyst in the paint), or they can be used without being catalyzed and clear-coated after application. If the urethane is clear-coated, the catalyst is added to the clear coat.

Special Tools for Striping at Home

Novice pinstripers can't be expected to pull a straight line like the professionals. For amateur pinstripers, a couple of tools and techniques can make the job much easier.

One tool to use is the Beugler, a pinstriping machine that comes complete with all the accessories you might need. Think of it as a small paint wheel, constantly supplied with fresh paint, that you roll along the side of your car. With a little practice,

What you need to get started: a roll of tape, Prepsol for cleaning, and your paint.

The first step before starting a pinstripe job is a good wash job, and then the car should be wiped down with Prepsol.

Use the Prepsol to wipe down the area that will be pinstriped. The Prepsol will remove any lingering wax, dirt, and (hopefully) silicones.

Eric Aurand lays down the tape nice and straight, following the contours of the Deuce body.

the line you leave behind will be consistent and straight, done without the bother of applying masking tape.

The Beugler comes as a kit, consisting of the basic body (or paint reservoir), a series of wheel heads, a roll of magnetic tape, and an assortment of guide rods. The wheel head contains the little wheel that runs along the side of the car, and each head has a wheel of a different width. The wider the wheel, the wider the line (pretty complicated science here), from ultra thin to fat and hairy.

To get started, you pull off the head, pull back the plunger, and fill the body with paint. Though you need to thin the paint you apply with a brush, the Beugler works best when filled with paint straight from the can. Next, attach the head with the appropriate wheel to create a line as wide as you need. Before heading directly to the car, however,

there is one more important step.

Creating a straight line means following a guide. Included in the Beugler kit is a roll of magnetic tape. Before starting across the car with the Beugler full of paint, you must lay the magnetic tape across the body. This is your guide. Lay the tape across the car, bend it to follow the body lines, and then stand back and make sure it runs straight and smooth. Then mount one of the guide rods in the Beugler and let the guide rod run along the edge of the magnetic tape as you pull the Beugler along toward you.

The magnetic tape obviously doesn't work so well with fiberglass or steel bodies with a lot of bondo under the paint. In order to avoid scratching the paint, you will have to be sure the tape is wiped clean before you stick it to the car.

Depending on the design and placement of the stripes on your car, the reveal lines might be used in

It is important to be sure the tape is well stuck to the body so no paint can migrate under the tape and spoil your perfect paint job.

place of the magnetic tape. In this case, you need to choose a guide rod that puts the Beugler the correct distance away from the reveal, and then just pull the Beugler toward you as you would if using the magnetic tape as the guide. Reposition the guide rod, and you can go back and add a second line in a second color, parallel to the first.

Like any other tool, the Beugler works best when it's kept clean. After each use you need to strip the whole thing down to the bare body and immerse it in the thinner of your choice. Failure to clean it thoroughly will result in a plunger that is stuck permanently in the body.

For first-time pinstripers there is another tool that makes the job of pinstriping much easier. This product is a special masking tape called 3M Fine Line Striping Tape.

Think of it as six or eight thin strips of masking tape on one roll. You put the wide masking tape on straight and smooth. Next, you pull out one of the small strips which leaves an opening ready for paint with masking tape on either side of it. If you need a heavier line, just pull two of the "pull-outs." This is a good product for the home striper. In fact, some of the professional stripers use this tape in tough situations.

If this tape has a down side, it is the tape's inability to flex. Anything more than a mild curve will have to be done freehand, or with two pieces of 3M plastic tape laid out side by side, with a space between them equal to the width of one pinstripe.

If the design is simple and nearly straight, you can just put on the tape, pull out one strip, and apply the paint. The key to success is making sure the car is

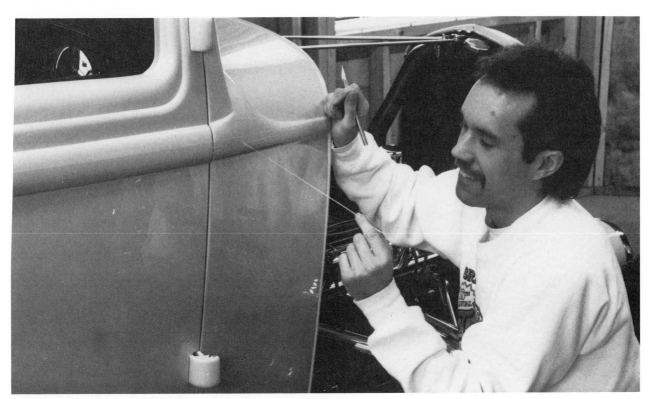

After making sure the tape has adhered to the car, pull out one pull-out and get ready to lay down the first line.

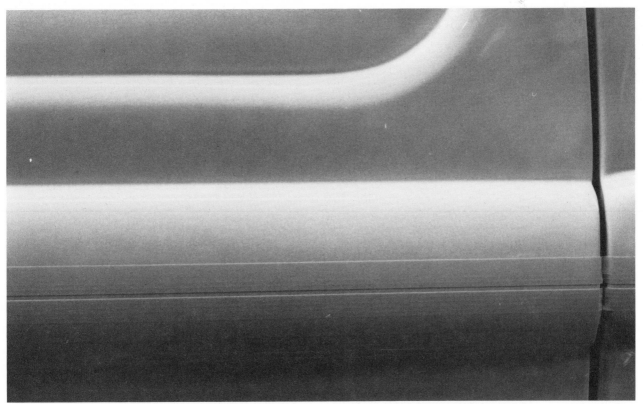

A close-up of the door after one pull-out is removed. Users should be careful at seams and door breaks so the tape makes complete contact with the body; otherwise, these areas will have to be touched up later.

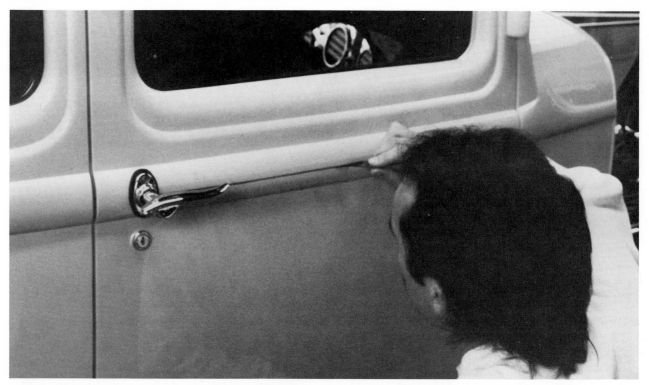

Eric lays down a pinstripe. As in freehand pinstriping, the brush is a special camel or squirrel hair brush designed for pinstriping and sign painting.

The brush is always pulled toward the painter. Though it's much easier with the Fine Line Tape, the painter still needs to be neat and needs to thin the paint to the right consistency.

Eric, an illustrator and graphic artist by trade, feels that two stripes in different colors make a much better design, so a second pull out is removed.

A close-up of the tape after one pinstripe is finished and before the second pinstripe is added. The multiple pull-outs allow the user to choose multiple stripes or two stripes of different widths.

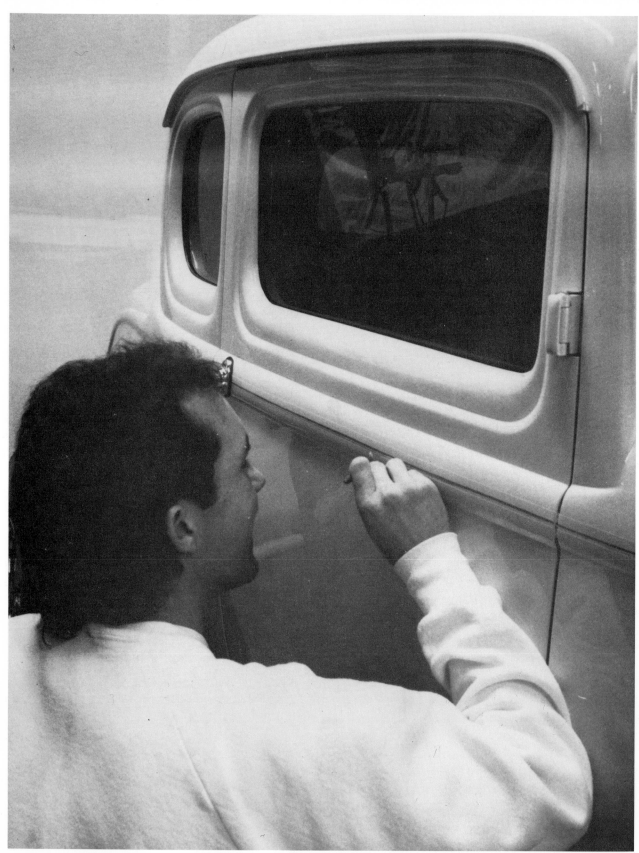

Eric pulls another line, the second pinstripe in a second color, across the Deuce door.

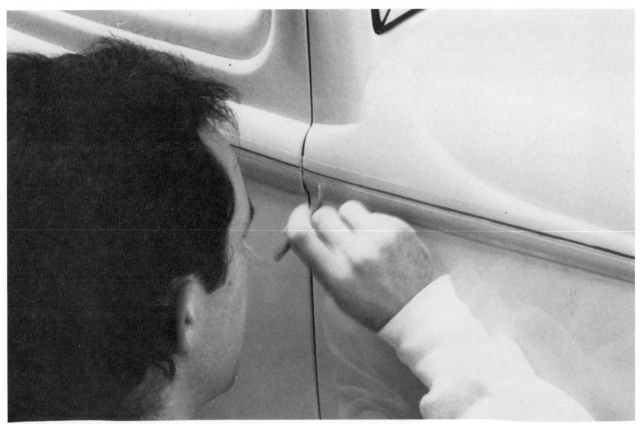

Choosing the second color is sometimes difficult. You need a color that works with both the car's body color and the color of the first pinstripe. The PMS book is especially useful in finding two colors for the pinstripes.

clean, making sure the tape goes on straight, and making sure the tape sticks. Once the tape is applied, pull one pull-out, and use your new brush to pull a nice line. It's a good idea to push down both edges of the tape as you move along. The second "pull out" can be removed after the first color is applied. Now just put on the second color and pull off the tape.

Just Do It!

Laying down a nice line is a special skill acquired after considerable practice. Brian Truesdell, a pin-striper since 1974, suggests that beginners use 3M tape or a special tool like the Beugler until they have considerable experience. He also stresses the important role that preparation plays in a good striping job.

Before applying the tape or trying to lay down a line, the surface must be clean—*very clean.* A cleaning solvent called Prepsol is commonly used by professional stripers (after a very thorough wash job) to remove any old wax or any film on the paint. Special sign painter's Prepsol is available for problem areas.

One of the biggest headaches for a striper is removing waxes and polishes that contain silicones. Some people apply a little of the striping paint on a small area of the body before the actual striping begins. If the new paint "fish-eyes," then more cleaning is needed. In a worst-case situation, fish-eye eliminator can be added to the striping paint (although it does weaken the striping paint).

Once the surface is ultra clean, the striping can begin. If you use the 3M tape, you have the option of one or two lines of various sizes. The design will depend on the style you've chosen for the car and your personal taste. When in doubt, remember that less is more (thin lines generally look more professional than fat ones). Besides, you can add to the striping later. With the multiple pull-outs of the 3M tape, you can easily run two parallel lines of different colors along the contours of the quarter panel and doors.

Laying down a nice, consistent line is largely dependent on learning how to correctly thin the paint. You need the right consistency so the brush puts on a nice, even line. Thin the paint too much, and the line spreads and has no definition. Thin it too little, and the line is dry, with bare spots where no paint was transferred from the brush to the surface. As a starting point, Brian suggests you try one part paint to one-quarter part thinner. Always pull the brush toward you, never move it across or away from you.

A close-up of the door after the second color is added. Sometimes a little touch-up is needed at the edges like this. It all depends on how careful you were in applying the tape.

Any of the regular striping paints like these can be used with the Beugler pinstriping tool.

Brian Truesdell uses the small, three-ounce Dixie cups for the paint mixing. (Larger cups have a wax coating that mixes with and contaminates the paint in the cup.)

Once you think you've got the paint mixed to the correct consistency, brush some on a small white card to "feel" how thick the paint is and how the brush drags as it moves across the card. Brian takes his paint from the card instead of from the little cup. Dragging the brush across the card allows him to check the thickness of the paint and also helps to keep the brush in its correct shape. If the paint refuses to flow correctly, a little linseed oil can be added as a thinner. This has no effect on the paint itself other than to slightly slow the drying time.

You're probably thinking, "What if I make a mistake?" Mistakes, at least fresh ones, can be wiped off with a rag. Even the next day, One-Shot or Chromatic enamel can usually be taken off with thinner and a clean rag. When using the urethanes, however, you have to be more careful because they adhere with more tenacity to the surface being painted.

Brian offered the following list of helpful hints for the first-time pinstriper:

● Any time the stripes are laid down over a fresh paint job, such as one that's only a few hours old, the striping paint tends to stick better and quicker to the paint underneath, leaving less time to wipe off mistakes. When pinstripes are to be laid down over a fresh urethane paint job, the urethane should dry for two or three days first. Otherwise the

To fill the body of the Beugler, pull back the plunger and fill the cavity. Unlike paint applied by hand, you don't want to thin the paint you put in the body.

tape applied over the fresh paint job may cause the urethane to wrinkle.

● If you chose to do it yourself with the help of the 3M tape, it's critical to make sure the tape sticks correctly. Run your thumb or forefinger along the tape just before applying the paint to ensure that the edges are really stuck down.

● With plastic or fiberglass surfaces, static electricity can be a problem. The simple cure is to wipe the surface down with a damp rag prior to painting.

● The key to a good striping job is to choose good color combinations, keep your design simple, and take your time. This is definitely a case where haste makes waste.

Conclusion

Though probably not considered part of "detailing" in the strictest sense, pinstriping is an area where a few details make a lot of difference. With a few helpful tools and a little practice on that old hood behind the garage, there is no reason you can't do the pinstriping yourself.

The Beugler kit includes the body, a number of paint heads for different size stripes, a roll of magnetic tape, and a series of guide rods.

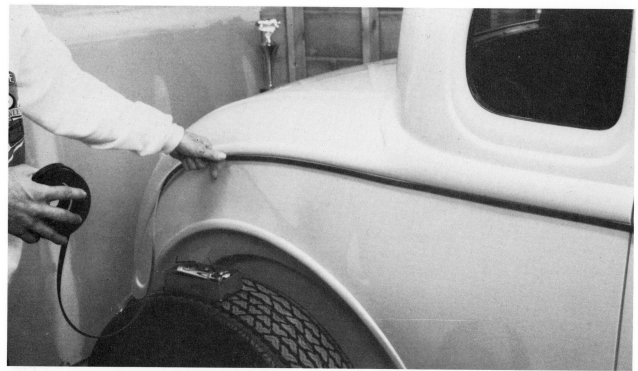

The roll of magnetic tape can be run across the car to act as a guide for the Beugler tool. Be sure to wipe off the back side of the magnetic tape to prevent scratching the paint.

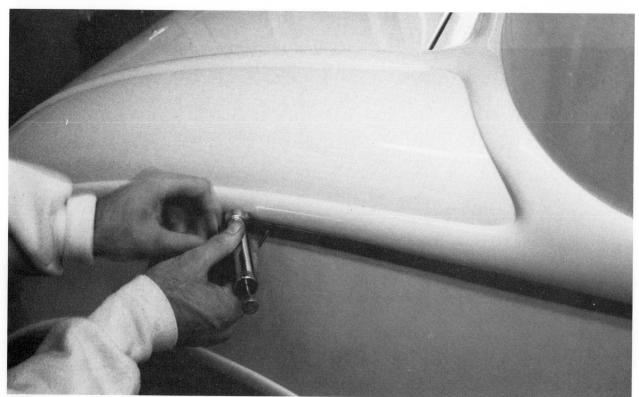

Before actually starting to paint, you must choose the guide rod that puts the Beugler and the pinstripe where you want it. Here we test and adjust the guide rod.

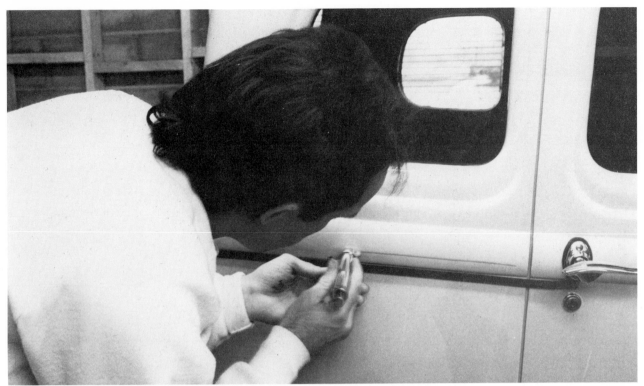

Ready, set, go. The Beugler rolls out a perfect pinstripe, following the path laid out by the magnetic tape. Depend- *ing on the position of the guide rod, it can be hard to start the pinstripe right at the edge of the door or body.*

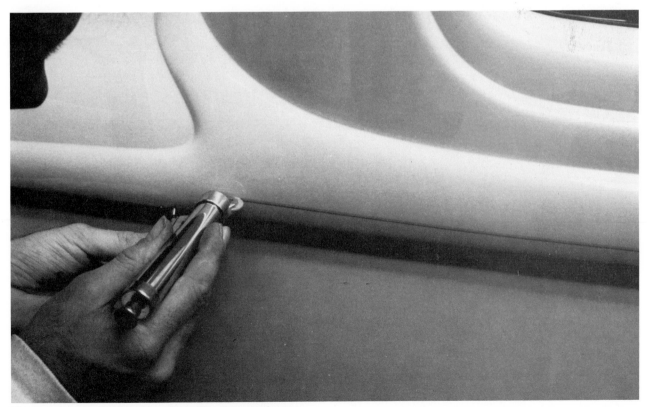

The key to a good job is the preparation. Lay out the tape carefully and keep the tool moving nice and steady.

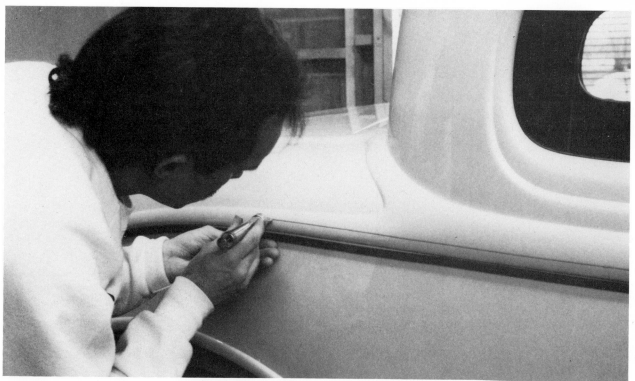

With a little practice, the paint goes on as easy as you please. You might get so good other people will pay you to pinstripe their cars. A new career is just around the corner

If the pinstripes are designed to follow the contours of the body, and if the reveal lines are as strong as those on this Deuce, you can use the tool without the magnetic tape.

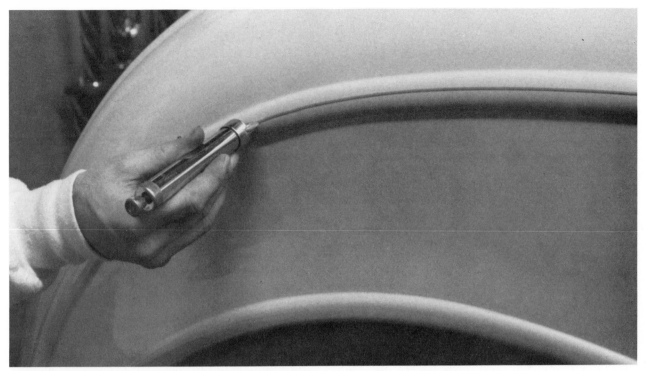

Eliminating the magnetic tape means choosing a guide rod that will follow a natural seam or reveal, one that puts the roller where you want the stripe to be.

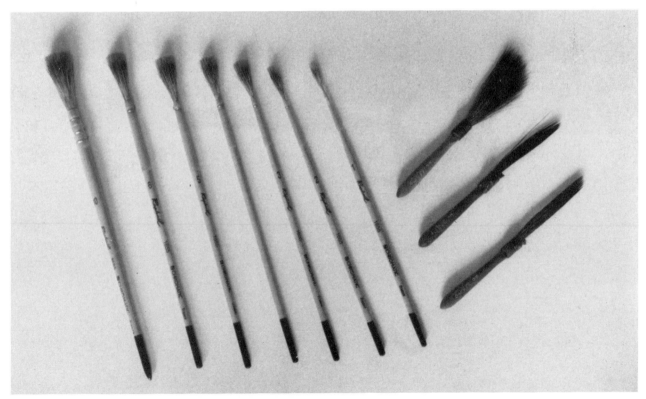

Tools of the trade. On the left are sign painter's brushes, and on the right are three of the long-bristle pinstriping brushes.

Chapter 8

Two-Hour Detail

Introduction

The two-hour detail may not be a true detail at all. The purist may insist that his street rod be detailed completely or not at all. Yet the real world seems to create numerous occasions when the car must be clean and you just don't have a whole day to spend doing a complete detailing job.

We might like to spend an entire day detailing the hot rod or street rod. But what is a person to do when the show opens tomorrow and today's schedule is plum full? What about when it's all you can do just to get to Back to the 50s, or Indy, or the Nats or whatever, much less find time to really detail the car before leaving town?

This chapter is written to help you do a really good cleanup when time is short. The ideas presented here are intended to provide some help for those all-too-common occasions when you are forced to take some shortcuts in cleaning and detailing your car. Maybe it isn't really a detailing process but rather a matter of making the best use of two hours spent cleaning the car.

Start With the Body

Though some rodders and detailers start with the engine when they do a complete detailing job, in this situation it's easier to start with the body. The

The best laid plans . . . Little rainstorms like this are the reason why you need to have a plan for a two-hour detailing. Rodder's Digest

Even without a storm, shows always create the need for extra cleaning, if for no other reason than your desire to make the car look as good as it can. Rodder's Digest

equipment you need is pretty much the same equipment you would use for a complete detailing job: a long hose, a nozzle for the end of the hose, some shade for the car, car-wash soap, a wash mitt, and plenty of clean cotton towels. (Don't take them from the hotel room or you risk an extra charge when you check out.)

Wash the car as you always do, starting with a thorough rinse of the entire vehicle to flush off as much grit as possible. Wash one small area at a time and rinse that area before going on to the next part of the car. Although you don't want to be too sloppy, some of the detailing tricks can probably be saved for another occasion. You want the car clean, but you may not want to work the paintbrush into the grille bars or use the toothbrush on the Ford or Chevy logo.

After the wash job is finished, flush the entire car one more time to remove any lingering soap. Wipe

off the car in two steps as outlined earlier. Don't skimp here, or the water you fail to wipe off will evaporate and leave little reminders behind. When the car has been wiped off, open all the doors and wipe off the doorjambs with a damp towel. Open the hood too and clean the edge of the hood and the inner fender lips.

Because time is short, you probably don't have time for a complete polish and wax job. There are a couple of alternatives open to you. Some street rodders will use their favorite polish or glaze product on the entire body to get the paint really clean and then skip the wax coat. A better alternative might be a cleaner/wax; that way the paint will get a nice shine and still be protected until the next time you do a true detailing job.

All the normal rules of waxing apply. Work on one small area at a time and use a fresh applicator or towel if possible. Don't wait for the wax to dry, just

The equipment needs for a two-hour detailing are nearly the same as for a full-blown, all-day affair.

A vacuum cleaner is still the best way to get the dirt out of the mats and carpet.

wipe it off while it's still wet. Try not to get any wax in seams or at the edges of doors and windows. No one will notice that there isn't any wax right at that edge, and you will save the time needed to clean all those edges and seams with a toothbrush. When the quick wax job is finished, walk around the entire car and look for any obvious wax build-up or areas that were missed while waxing.

The Engine

A complete engine detailing is out of the question. It's messy and time-consuming. Instead, just wipe off the most obvious dirt with a damp towel or sponge and then follow with a little polish or wax. Pay attention to the big things: the top of the radiator, the air cleaner, the valve covers, the top of the headers, and the upper part of the firewall.

A quick wipe-down with the cleaner/wax will make the chrome valve covers shine, and the same holds true for most air cleaners. Anyone who takes a quick peek under the hood will only see the sparkle from the shiny chrome.

The Interior

Cleaning the interior always starts with a good vacuuming, no matter how much detailing you intend to do. Pull out the mats, slap them against the pavement to loosen any dirt, and then vacuum them. When the mats are clean start on the carpet and move onto the seats, taking time to get in the crevices and the back seat, too. While you're down there, vacuum the dust and dirt off the console and from around the shifter boot.

Don't neglect the dashboard; it's too big an area to skip. Wipe the dashboard down with a damp cloth, and be sure to include the top of the steering column and the face of the gauges. The dash should probably receive a little true detailing as well. Maybe a quick once-over with the cleaner/wax for a metal dash, or an application of dressing for a vinyl or leather dashboard.

The inside glass is next. Wash it with your favorite cleanser and some clean towels. The window cranks and door hardware are pretty obvious parts of the interior, so be sure to wipe down all these parts

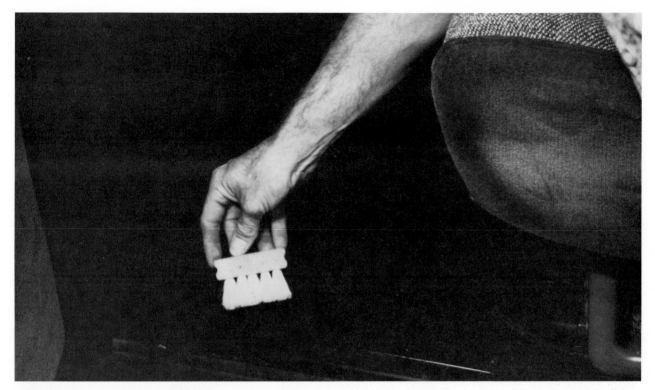

When you're on the road, a small brush can take the place of the vacuum if things aren't too dirty.

To save time, visible chassis members should be washed with the rest of the car and then wiped down with a little cleaner/wax after the car has been dried.

You can always tell the street rodders who are too lazy to do any detailing by the special suede cars (or trucks) they drive. Rodder's Digest

as you move around the interior washing the inside glass.

As you step out of the car, take one last look at the doorjambs to be sure they're clean.

The Chassis

No, you don't want to crawl underneath the car and completely detail the chassis. If someone at the show wants to do the reptile-slither and discover your less-than-perfect chassis, it's just too bad. The idea is to get those most obvious areas as clean as you can as quickly as you can.

If yours is a fat-fendered car, then most or all of the chassis parts are down there where they're hard

to see. If they're real hard to see, maybe you should just let them go and spend the time on another part of the car. Owners of hiboys and early cars will have to spend at least some time on the obvious things like the front axle and, maybe, the front suspension.

Most of these parts were probably washed with the body. If not, give the inner fenders, front axle, and maybe the backing plates a quick wash job with a strong soap-and-water solution. Wipe everything off and go over the chrome-plated goodies with cleaner/wax before doing the final wipe-down.

At the rear, the amount of work you do depends, once again, on how much of the chassis and suspension is hangin' out there for everyone to see. It's a matter of washing the most visible parts of the suspension and following that with a little polish or cleaner/wax.

Tires and Wheels

Though the idea here is a quick detailing job, the wheels and tires form a big part of the car's appearance. We need a compromise, a way to obtain a good finished product without going through the complete detailing process.

Because we aren't going to crawl under the car to fully detail the chassis, we won't be jacking up the car. Because the car won't be jacked up, the easiest way to save time on tire and wheel detailing is by doing the work with the tires and wheels left on the car.

The initial washing of the tires and wheels can be done when the body is washed. If the front tires and wheels still aren't clean, wash them down with soap and water or a general-purpose tire cleaner to remove any accumulation of brake dust. Polishing the wheels can be fairly time consuming and can probably be eliminated here. Just make sure each wheel is clean and wipe it dry. The rear wheels are probably cleaner than the front ones and may only need to be wiped off with a damp rag followed by a dry terry cloth towel. (The rears usually don't have any brake dust on them.)

As a final touch, aluminum wheels can be wiped down with a little WD-40 on a rag to give them a nice shine. Chrome wheels can be wiped down with a towel and some cleaner/wax.

The tires are probably pretty clean after you've finished washing the car body and the wheels, so you can skip the actual tire cleaning operation. Wipe the tires dry with clean terry cloth towels and then settle for an application of tire dressing. Use your favorite product to give the tires the correct degree of blackness. Because the tires and wheels are on the car, be careful with whatever you use on the tires so you don't spray it all over the fender or the wheel. The use of an applicator or a sponge will keep the dressing confined to the tires.

When You're All Through

When you're all through, what you have is a nice, clean car. No, it hasn't really been detailed. Of course, most people won't see the difference. The idea is to get the car as clean as you can as often as you can.

The actual emphasis you choose when you do a two-hour detail may differ slightly from that outlined here. Like the full detailing, you need to find a washing and cleaning sequence that fits your car and your circumstances.

The two-hour detail is intended to help you make your car look very good on those occasions when you simply don't have a full day to do the work. You want a car you don't have to apologize for, and when you've finished with this shortened detailing sequence, you won't have to.

The people at Meguiar's have designed a quick detailer to provide your car with that "just waxed" look in only about ten minutes. Just spray it on and wipe it off.

If you never let the engine get too dirty, all it needs is to be wiped down with a towel and treated to a little polish and some cleaner/wax on the chrome components.

Chassis parts that are as obvious as the rear end, shocks, and panhard bar on Doug's Deuce will have to be cleaned and treated to a little polish and wax during the two-hour detailing.

For the detailer or street rodder in a hurry, Meguiar's makes a cleaner and wax in their non-professional line, as well as a number of glaze and polish products in the professional line, that can be wiped on and wiped off as a one-step operation.

Don't waste your detailing efforts by driving your rod on a dusty or muddy road, or by parking it in a spot where it will get dirty. Parking it on the grass, as shown here, is fine, but avoid areas that are potentially muddy or dusty.

Liquid Lustre is a popular one-step cleaner/wax product sold at many car shows and used by many street rod and custom car owners.

Once you've got your rod's interior clean, keep it that way. Keep it free of personal belongings, food and film wrappers, detailing equipment, jackets, and other items so people can appreciate your efforts. Keep your belongings in the trunk or in bags you can remove from your car, and throw your trash away. Rodder's Digest

Stickers, badges, and magnets from clubs, shows, and meets are fun, but they can detract from your car's look and from your detailing effort. This dash and windshield look great and they'll stay that way without any stickers or badges. If you're going to stick a badge or sticker somewhere, make sure you really want it there. Rodder's Digest

Safe Disposal and Recycling of Parts and Chemicals

One of the most difficult problems in repairing or restoring any vehicle is the question of what to do with the old parts and poisonous fluids you inevitably generate. Everybody knows these days that two of our largest environmental concerns are the related ills of landfill overuse and groundwater contamination. Unfortunately, our interest in environmental problems far outstrips our current ability to find answers to them.

While repairing or restoring your vehicle, there are several components and fluids that can actually be recycled, such as batteries, motor oil, electrical components, brake pads, and more. Take advantage of the recycling effort.

There are many more components and fluids that cannot be recycled, however. The best you can do with these hazardous wastes is to control the spread of the hazard. Check with your local pollution control agency or your county government for hazardous waste collection sites where you can dispose of these parts and fluids.

Parts

Actual pieces of mechanical junk are generally more of a pain than a danger to dispose of. Assuming that the pieces aren't filled with fluid or particularly greasy, metal parts will sit happily inert in a landfill and actually decompose over time—albeit a long, long time. Yet, some plastic and rubber pieces release a number of carcinogenic chemicals as they decompose. If possible, you should bring big metal parts to a local junkyard; often yards will accept these pieces for their scrap value and sometimes melt them down to be recycled.

Batteries

Old vehicle batteries are like environmental time bombs just waiting to explode. The average vehicle battery contains more than 18lb of toxic metals, and the chemicals inside can burst through the plastic shell or seep through cracks and leak onto your floor. And everyone has one or two old batteries laying around in a corner of their garage or workshop.

Fortunately, batteries are easy to dispose of and the cores can be recycled by the manufacturers to make new batteries. In many states, shops that sell batteries are required by law to accept old batteries free of charge and see to their safe disposal. Some responsible shops even reinforce this by giving you a rebate when buying a new battery if you bring in the old battery.

Tires

Tires are a well-known dumping hazard, and methods for their disposal have been well-developed in almost every state. In the past when you went to dispose of your old tires at a tire shop or landfill, the typical response was to say that you can't dump your tires there, which is ultimately the wrong answer, since many people just get frustrated and toss them by the side of the road or in vacant lots.

Most states today have mandatory tire buy-back laws for dealers and shops. These laws typically have regulations that require tire dealers to accept used tires for disposal, usually with a small fee attached.

Electrical Components

Core parts of many electrical components can be recycled by the manufacturers to build new units. Alternators, generators, starter motors, and other electrical components fall into this category, and many shops will offer a rebate on your new part when you bring in the old one for recycling. Take advantage of such an arrangement.

Brake Pads

Brake pad cores can also be recycled by the manufacturers, and in many states, shops that sell pads are required by law to accept old pads free of charge and see to their recycling or safe disposal. This is especially important with nonmetallic, asbestos brake pads since asbestos is a powerful carcinogen.

When replacing asbestos pads, never blow away old brake dust with your face nearby as it simply provides you with easy-to-inhale airborne asbestos dust. Instead, use a moist cloth to wipe it away and dispose of the cloth.

Exhaust System Components

Not surprisingly, all of the exhaust system components that you route the engine exhaust through become caked with carcinogens and pollutants over time. The only way to safely dispose of used exhaust pipes, mufflers, and catalytic converters is to bring them to a hazardous waste collection site or to contact your local pollution control agency for other alternative sites.

Fluids

The best rule of thumb as you work with chemicals and fluids is to remember that if you can smell it, it's bad news. And the stronger the odor, the more dangerous it is—both to your immediate health and to the atmosphere and groundwater. Cleaners, paints, and all oil-derived liquids are the big things to watch out for. Dumped carelessly by the wayside, these toxic chemicals will quickly work their way into the water cycle and return to haunt us all.

The easiest solution, of course, is not to generate any more of these wastes than necessary in the first place. Except for motor oil, the greatest volume of volatile chemicals is generated by cleaning, not the actual changing of a car's fluids. It's best to start off with the mildest cleaners possible at first—soap and water can, in fact, do a lot of work—not just for the environment's sake but because these are also the easiest on the vehicle itself.

You will inevitably generate some hazardous material no matter what you do, however. Things like spray cleaners and naptha, for example—real health and environmental nightmares—are just too convenient to realistically swear off of completely. The trick is simply to catch as much of these fluids as possible after use, and to keep them tightly covered in plastic, glass, or metal containers until you can safely get rid of them. Leaving pans of cleaners uncovered sends these toxins directly into the atmosphere through evaporation, so keep them covered at all times.

Caked grease and ruined rags should also be kept tightly wrapped up in a cool place and disposed of along with actual fluids—they're simply volatiles that are currently trapped in solid form. And beware of the fire hazard of these rags.

All toxins should be kept separated since cross contamination simply makes the disposal issue more complicated.

Motor Oil

Used motor oil poses a great threat to the environment—and to yourself, as it contains carcinogens. Many states prohibit putting used motor oil in the trash or disposing of it in landfills.

Fortunately, however, motor oil can be recycled and used as fuel for ships, furnaces, and other things. In many states, shops that sell oil or provide oil changes are required by law to collect used motor oil for recycling.

Some counties offer curbside recycling of used motor oil, so check with your county government. These recycling programs sometimes have strict rules on how the used oil must be stored if they will take it for recycling; some want it stored only in plastic containers while others require glass jars, so be sure to ask.

You must also be certain to keep your used motor oil pure and not mix it with other fluids for disposal. If the used oil is contaminated with even minute traces of brake fluid or coolant, the entire batch in the collection tank will be ruined.

Antifreeze and Coolant

The main ingredient in antifreeze and coolants is ethylene glycol, a chemical that can be reconditioned in wastewater treatment systems. Small amounts of used antifreeze—1 gallon or so—can thus be safely disposed of in your home's sanitary sewer system when mixed with large amounts of water.

You should never dispose of antifreeze in storm sewers or septic systems as these do not run through the wastewater treatment system and the ethylene glycol will eventually contaminate the groundwater. Antifreeze dumped into a septic system will also destroy the bacteria in the system that septic tanks rely on to operate.

Parts Cleaners

The old-fashioned parts cleaner fluids that worked like magic in removing years of oil and grime from your vehicle parts also removed layers of your own skin and seeped directly into your liver, where they definitely didn't do you any good. When disposing of these old parts cleaners, first read the label on the container. If the product is labelled as being flammable, combustible , or contains any solvents such as petroleum distillates or aromatic hydrocarbons, then it must be disposed of at a hazardous waste collection site.

If the product is a liquid and does not contain any solvents, it can usually be disposed of in a sanitary sewer system after being mixed with large quantities of water. Never pour it down a storm sewer or into a septic system since the liquids will not be treated but will instead seep directly into our groundwater.

Today several alternative parts cleaners are readily available and easy on you and the environment while still scrubbing away all the oil and grease. Check them out.

There is also one other option: Never underestimate the power of hot water, soap, and scrubbing.

Gasoline

Gasoline is one of the most dangerous fluids around your house or workshop because it is extremely volatile.

Often times, most waste gas is either contaminated or old. If it has been contaminated with paint or other soluble contaminants, it cannot be reconditioned. Check with your county for a hazardous waste collection site.

Stale gas can be used after adding one of the many reconditioning agents on the market. However, many people prefer not to risk their vehicle's engine and use the stale gas in a lawn mower or other small gas engine instead.

Sources

Eastwood Company
580 Lancaster Avenue
Box 296
Malvern, PA 19355

Eastwood is well known for their great catalog of tools and equipment intended for serious auto builders and rebuilders. Some of the products in the new catalog are well suited to anyone interested in detailing his or her car.

Meguiar's Inc.
17991 Mitchell South
Irvine, CA 92714

Meguiar's has been in the business of supplying car care products to both the professional and the enthusiast since the beginning of the century. They make a wide variety of products that are respected by people in the field.

B.T. Design
Attn: Brian Truesdell
937 Smith Avenue
St. Paul, MN

Boyd's Car Care Products
c/o Boyd's Wheels
8402 Cerritos Avenue
Stanton, CA 90680

Boyd's Car Care Products were developed with the help of a certain Far-Out street rod detailer.

One Grand Products Inc.
13820 Saticoy
Van Nuys, CA 91402

One Grand makes a variety of detailing products, from paint cleaner to their Blitz Wax. For less than $20, One Grand will send out a kit with all the products necessary to detail one car—as a means of inducing people unfamiliar with the products to give them a try.

Eagle One
2231 Faraday Avenue
Carlsbad, CA 92008

Eagle One makes a full line of car care products, including a very complete line of wheel and tire care products.

Mothers
5456 Industrial Drive
Huntington Beach, CA 92649

Mothers makes one of the best known polishes used by automotive enthusiasts. In addition to their well-known Mothers Mag & Aluminum polish, they now offer a complete line of car care products.

Lexol Products
PO Box 7329
Marietta, GA 30065

Lexol is a company that started out selling products for cleaning saddles and other horse gear. Their leather cleaner and leather conditioner are in wide use by professional and enthusiast detailers throughout the country.

House of Kolor
2521 27th Avenue South
Minneapolis, MN 55406

Jon Kosmoski's House of Kolor makes some of the best and brightest custom paint in the world, and the only urethane pinstriping paint.

Index